AN EXEGETICAL SUMMARY OF
JUDE

AN EXEGETICAL SUMMARY OF JUDE

Second Edition

J. Harold Greenlee

SIL International

Second Edition
© 1999, 2008 by SIL International

Library of Congress Catalog Card Number: 2008923516
ISBN: 978-155671-190-9

Printed in the United States of America

All Rights Reserved
No part of this publication may be reproduced, stored in a retrieval system, or transmitted in any form or by any means without the express permission of SIL International. However, brief excerpts, generally understood to be within the limits of fair use, may be quoted without written permission.

Copies of this and other publications
of SIL International may be obtained from

International Academic Bookstore
SIL International
7500 West Camp Wisdom Road
Dallas, TX 75236-5699, USA

Voice: 972-708-7404
Fax: 972-708-7363
academic_books@sil.org
www.ethnologue.com

PREFACE

Exegesis is concerned with the interpretation of a text. Exegesis of the New Testament involves determining the meaning of the Greek text. Translators must be especially careful and thorough in their exegesis of the New Testament in order to accurately communicate its message in the vocabulary, grammar, and literary devices of another language. Questions occurring to translators as they study the Greek text are answered by summarizing how scholars have interpreted the text. This is information that should be considered by translators as they make their own exegetical decisions regarding the message they will communicate in their translations.

The Semi-Literal Translation

As a basis for discussion, a semi-literal translation of the Greek text is given so that the reasons for different interpretations can best be seen. When one Greek word is translated into English by several words, these words are joined by hyphens. There are a few times when clarity requires that a string of words joined by hyphens have a separate word, such as "not" (μή), inserted in their midst. In this case, the separate word is surrounded by spaces between the hyphens. When alternate translations of a Greek word are given, these are separated by slashes.

The Text

Variations in the Greek text are noted under the heading TEXT. The base text for the summary is the text of the fourth revised edition of *The Greek New Testament,* published by the United Bible Societies, which has the same text as the twenty-sixth edition of the *Novum Testamentum Graece* (Nestle-Aland). The versions that follow different variations are listed without evaluating their choices.

The Lexicon

The meaning of a key word in context is the first question to be answered. Words marked with a raised letter in the semi-literal translation are treated separately under the heading LEXICON. First, the lexicon form of the Greek word is given. Within the parentheses following the Greek word is the location number where, in the author's judgment, this word is defined in the *Greek-English Lexicon of the New Testament Based on Semantic Domains* (Louw and Nida 1988). When a semantic domain includes a translation of the particular verse being treated, **LN** in bold type indicates that specific translation. If the specific reference for the verse is listed in *A Greek-English Lexicon of the New Testament and Other Early Christian Literature* (Bauer, Arndt, Gingrich, and Danker 1979), the outline location and page number is given. Then English equivalents of the Greek word are given to show how it is translated by commentators who offer their own translations of the whole text and, after a semicolon, all the versions in the list of abbreviations for translations. When reference is made to "all versions," it refers to only the versions in the list of translations. Sometimes further comments are made about the meaning of the word or the significance of a verb's tense, voice, or mood.

The Questions

Under the heading QUESTION, a question is asked that comes from examining the Greek text under consideration. Typical questions concern the identity of an implied actor or object of an event word, the antecedent of a pronominal reference, the connection indicated by a relational word, the meaning of a genitive construction, the meaning of figurative language, the function of a rhetorical question, the identification of an ambiguity, and the presence of implied information that is needed to understand the passage correctly. Background information is also considered for a proper understanding of a passage. Although not all implied information and background information is made explicit in a translation, it is important to consider it so that the translation will not be stated in such a way that prevents a reader from arriving at the proper interpretation. The question is answered with a summary of what commentators have said. If there are contrasting differences of opinion, the different interpretations are numbered and the commentaries that support each are listed. Differences that are not treated by many of the commentaries often are not numbered, but are introduced with a contrastive 'Or' at the beginning of the sentence. No attempt has been made to select which interpretation is best.

In listing support for various statements of interpretation, the author is often faced with the difficult task of matching the different terminologies used in commentaries with the terminology he has adopted. Sometimes he can only infer the position of a commentary from incidental remarks. This book, then, includes the author's interpretation of the views taken in the various commentaries. General statements are followed by specific statements, which indicate the author's understanding of the pertinent relationships, actors, events, and objects implied by that interpretation.

The Use of This Book

This book does not replace the commentaries that it summarizes. Commentaries contain much more information about the meaning of words and passages. They often contain arguments for the interpretations that are taken and they may have important discussions about the discourse features of the text. In addition, they have information about the historical, geographical, and cultural setting. Translators will want to refer to at least four commentaries as they exegete a passage. However, since no one commentary contains all the answers translators need, this book will be a valuable supplement. It makes more sources of exegetical help available than most translators have access to. Even if they had all the books available, few would have the time to search through all of them for the answers.

When many commentaries are studied, it soon becomes apparent that they frequently disagree in their interpretations. That is the reason why so many answers in this book are divided into two or more interpretations. The reader's initial reaction may be that all of these different interpretations complicate exegesis rather than help it. However, before translating a passage, a translator needs to know exactly where there is a problem of interpretation and what the exegetical options are.

ABBREVIATIONS AND BIBLIOGRAPHY

COMMENTARIES AND REFERENCE BOOKS

AB	Neyrey, Jerome H. *2 Peter, Jude*. The Anchor Bible, vol. 37C. New York: Doubleday, 1993.
Alf	Alford, Henry. *The Epistles of St. John and St. Jude, and The Revelation*. The Greek Testament, vol. 4, part 2. London: Rivingtons, 1861.
BAGD	Bauer, Walter. *A Greek-English Lexicon of the New Testament and Other Early Christian Literature*. Translated and adapted from the 5th German edition, 1958, by William F. Arndt and F. Wilbur Gingrich. 2d English ed. revised and augmented by F. Wilbur Gingrich and Frederick W. Danker. Chicago: University of Chicago Press, 1979.
Blm	Bloomfield, S. T. *The Greek Testament with English Notes*, vol. 2. London: Longman, Orme, Brown, Green & Longmans, 1839.
BNTC	Kelly, J. N. D. *The Epistles of Peter and of Jude*. Black's New Testament Commentary. Peabody, Mass.: Hendrickson Publishers, 1969.
CBC	Leaney, A. R. C. *The Letters of Peter and Jude*. The Cambridge Bible Commentary. Cambridge: The University Press, 1967.
EBC	Blum, Edwin A. "Jude." *The Expositor's Bible Commentary*, vol. 12. Grand Rapids: Zondervan, 1981.
EGT	Mayor, J. B. "The General Epistle of Jude." *The Expositor's Greek Testament*, vol. 5. New York: George H. Doran Co., n.d.
El	Plummer, Alfred. *The Epistles of St. Peter, St. John, and St. Jude*. Ellicott's New Testament Commentary. London: Cassell and Co., Ltd., n.d.
Hie	Hiebert, D. Edmond. *Second Peter and Jude*. Greenville, S. C.: Unusual Publications, 1989.
Hu	Huther, Joh. Ed., Th.D. *Critical and Exegetical Handbook to The General Epistles of James, Peter, John, and Jude*. English translation by Paton J. Gloag, D. B. Croom, and Clarke H. Irwin. New York: Funk & Wagnalls, 1887. Supplementary notes by Timothy Dwight, indicated by Hu(D).
ICC	Bigg, Charles. *The Epistles of St. Peter and St. Jude*. The International Critical Commentary, 2nd ed. Edinburgh: T. & T. Clark, 1910.
Law	Lawlor, George Lawrence. *The Epistle of Jude*. (no city): Presbyterian and Reformed Publishing Co., 1976.
Lg	Fronm3ller, C. F. C. "The General Epistle of Jude." *Commentary on the Holy Scriptures*, vol. 9, by John Peter Lange. Translated from the 2nd rev. German ed. by J. Isidor Mombert. Additional notes by J. Isidor Mombert, indicated by Lg(M).
LN	Louw, Johannes P., and Eugene A. Nida. *Greek-English Lexicon of the New Testament Based on Semantic Domains*. 2 vols. New York: United Bible Societies, 1988.
Lns	Lenski, R. C. H. *The Interpretation of The Epistles of St. Peter, St. John and St. Jude*. Columbus, Ohio: Wartburg Press, 1945.
NIBC	Hillyer, Norman. *1 and 2 Peter, Jude*. New International Biblical Commentary. Peabody, Mass.: Hendrickson Publishers, 1992
NTC	Kistemaker, Simon J. *Exposition of James, Epistles of John, Peter, and Jude*. New Testament Commentary Grand Rapids: Baker Books, 1996.
TBST	Lucas, Dick, and Christopher Green. *The Message of 2 Peter & Jude*. The Bible Speaks Today. Downers Grove, Ill.: Inter-Varsity Press, 1995.
TG	Bratcher, Robert G. *A Translator's Guide to the Letters from James, Peter, and Jude*. New York: United Bible Societies, 1984.

TH	Arichea, Daniel C., and Howard A. Hatton. *A Handbook on The Letter from Jude and The Second Letter from Peter*. UBS Handbook Series. New York: United Bible Societies, 1993.
TNTC	Green, Michael. *The Second Epistle General of Peter and the General Epistle of Jude*. Tyndale New Testament Commentaries, rev. ed. Grand Rapids: Eerdmans, 1996
WBC	Bauckham, Richard J. *Jude, 2 Peter*. Word Biblical Commentary, vol. 50. Waco, Tex.: Word Books, 1983.

GREEK TEXT AND TRANSLATIONS

GNT	The Greek New Testament. Edited by B. Aland, K. Aland, J. Karavidopoulos, C. Martini, and B. Metzger. 4th ed. London, New York: United Bible Societies, 1993.
CEV	The Holy Bible, Contemporary English Version. New York: American Bible Society, 1995.
ISV	The Holy Bible, International Standard Version. New Testament (Preview Release Edition). Yorba Linda, Cal.: Davidson Press, 1998.
KJV	The Holy Bible, Authorized (or King James) Version, 1611.
NAB	The New American Bible. Camden, New Jersey: Thomas Nelson, 1971.
NET	The NET Bible, New English Translation. www.NETBIBLE.ORG: Biblical Studies Press, L.L.C., 1998.
NIV	The Holy Bible, New International Version. Grand Rapids: Zondervan, 1984.
NJB	The New Jerusalem Bible. Garden City, New York: Doubleday, 1985.
NLT	The Holy Bible, New Living Translation. Wheaton, Ill.: Tyndale House, 1996.
NRSV	The Holy Bible, New Revised Standard Version. New York: Oxford University Press, 1989.
REB	The Revised English Bible. Oxford: Oxford University Press and Cambridge University Press, 1989.
TEV	Good News Bible, Today's English Version. 2d ed. New York: American Bible Society, 1992.
TNT	The Translator's New Testament. London: British and Foreign Bible Society, 1973.

GRAMMATICAL TERMS

act.	active	opt.	optative
fut.	future	pass.	passive
impera.	imperative	perf.	perfect
indic.	indicative	pres.	present
infin.	infinitive	subj.	subjunctive
mid.	middle		

EXEGETICAL SUMMARY OF JUDE

DISCOURSE UNIT: 1–25 [CBC; REB]. The topic is the danger of false belief.

DISCOURSE UNIT: 1–4 [CBC, Lg]. The topic is the greeting and reason for writing [CBC, Lg] and warning and exhortation [Lg].

DISCOURSE UNIT: 1–2 [AB, BNTC, EBC, EGT, GNT, Hie, Law, Lns, NTC, TBST, TNTC, WBC; CEV, ISV, NAB, NIV, NJB, NLT, TEV]. The topic is the introduction [TG; TEV], greetings from Jude [ISV, NLT], greeting [EBC, EGT, GNT, Hie, Lns, NTC; CEV, NAB], address [NIV, NJB], address and greeting [AB, BNTC, WBC], the author and his readers [TNTC], the common relationships of writer and readers [Law], Jude the obscure [TBST].

1 Jude, of-Jesus Christ slave,[a] and brother of James,

LEXICON—a. δοῦλος (LN 87.76) (BAGD 4. p. 206): 'slave' [BAGD, LN, Lns; NET, NLT], 'bondservant' [LN], 'servant' [AB, Alf, BNTC, WBC; all versions except NLT]. This word implies close and binding ties to the master [Hie], being bound to Jesus by love [Law], in a relationship closer than a brother [Hie], and stresses Jude's obedience and surrender to him [TH; NET]. It implies that he has part in the gospel ministry [Hie, Hu, TG], being involved in promoting the Word [Alf, BNTC, TH, WBC]. It indicates that Jude was a leader in the church [BNTC, Lg, TBST, TG, TH, WBC]. The absence of the definite article emphasizes the quality of servanthood [Law].

QUESTION—How is this epistle related to 2 Peter in view of the obvious similarity between the two?
  1. Jude was written before 2 Peter [AB, BNTC, CBC, EGT, TH, WBC] and 2 Peter expanded on Jude [CBC].
  2. 2 Peter was written before Jude [EBC, EI, Hie, ICC, Law, Lg, Lns].
  3. It is unlikely that one is copied from the other [NIBC, NTC, TNTC].

QUESTION—How are the two nouns related in the genitive construction Ἰησοῦ Χριστοῦ δοῦλος 'of Jesus Christ slave'?
  Δοῦλος 'slave' expresses the role relationship to the genitive 'Jesus Christ': related to Jesus Christ as a slave. The word order makes 'Jesus Christ' prominent [Hie]. It implies that he is writing what Jesus wants him to say [EBC]. He does not call himself the brother of Jesus because his physical relationship is subordinate to the spiritual relationship [Hu]. Modesty prevents him from calling himself the brother of Jesus [ICC, NIBC, WBC], but this is implied in the following phrase [ICC, Lns]. The author does not want to gain recognition by claiming to be a brother of Jesus [NTC; NET].

QUESTION—What relationship is indicated by δέ 'and'?
  It is not adversative, but introduces a different matter; the two expressed relationships are different [Hie].

QUESTION—How are the two nouns related in the genitive construction ἀδελφὸς Ἰακώβου 'brother of James'?

Ἀδελφός 'brother' expresses the role relationship to the genitive 'James': he is related to James as a brother. He is a brother of James and half-brother of Jesus [AB, BNTC, EBC, Hie, ICC, Law, Lg, NIBC, NTC, TBST, TNTC, WBC; NET]. His relationship to James is simply used for identification [WBC; NET], since Jude was a common name and two of Jesus' disciples had the same name [NET]. The name Ἰούδας is translated 'Judas' in Mark 3:19 and 'Judah' in Matthew 1:2–3 [TG], and only here it is traditionally translated 'Jude' to distinguish him from the betrayer, Judas [NET]. The mention that James was his brother adds authority to what he has to say [Hie]. James is the author of the Epistle of James [BNTC, CBC, EBC, Law, Lg, NTC, TBST]. This implies that Jude has authority in the church [BNTC, TH], but regarded his position to be inferior to that of James [Law, TNTC].

to-the called[a] (ones), in[b] God (the) Father loved[c] and Jesus Christ kept[d];

TEXT—Instead of ἠγαπημένοις 'loved', some manuscripts read ἠγιασμένοις 'sanctified'. GNT reads ἠγαπημένοις 'loved' with an A decision, indicating that the text is certain. Only Blm, Lg (but not Lg(M), and KJV read ἠγιασμένοις 'sanctified'.

LEXICON—a. κλητός (LN 33.314) (BAGD p. 436): 'called' [AB, Alf, BAGD, BNTC, LN, Lns, WBC; ISV, KJV, NET, NIV, NJB, NRSV], 'called by God' [NAB], 'chosen' [CEV]. The phrase τοῖς κλητοῖς 'the called ones' is translated 'those whom God has called' [REB, TNT] 'those who have been called by God' [TEV], 'all who are called' [NLT]. It refers to all Christians [El, Hie, Hu], to believers of every generation [NIBC]. It means being drawn to the Gospel by God [Alf, Law, Lg, TH], a personal experience [BNTC]; it stresses God's initiative [Hie]. This word is a virtual synonym for 'Christian' [BNTC, CBC, EBC, Hie, TG, TH, WBC]. It is the principal word of the phrase [Law, Lg].

b. ἐν with dative object (LN 83.13, 90.6) (BAGD I.3. p. 258): 'in' [Alf, BNTC, LN (83.13), Lns, WBC; NAB, NLT, NRSV, REB, TEV], 'in the presence of, before' [BAGD], 'wrapped in' [NET], 'by' [LN (90.6); CEV, ISV, KJV, NIV], not explicit [AB; NJB, TNT],

c. perf. pass. participle of ἀγαπάω (LN 25.43) (BAGD 1.d. p. 5): 'to be loved' [BAGD, LN, Lns, WBC; CEV, ISV, NIV], 'to be beloved' [AB, Alf, BNTC; NRSV], 'to find love' [NAB], 'to be dear' [NJB]; different text [KJV]. The passive voice is also translated as active with God as subject: 'to love' [TNT]. With ἐν 'in', it is translated 'to live in love' [NLT, REB, TEV], 'to be wrapped in love' [NET]. The perfect tense indicates a continued state [BNTC, Hie, Law, NTC, TH, WBC] resulting from a past action [Hie, Law, Lns, NIBC].

d. perf. pass. participle of τηρέω (LN 13.32, 37.122) (BAGD 2.b. p. 815): 'to be kept' [AB, Alf, LN (13.32), Lns, WBC; NET, NIV], 'to be kept safe' [BNTC; CEV, ISV, NJB, NRSV, REB], 'to be preserved' [KJV], 'to be guarded' [LN (37.122)], 'to be guarded safely' [NAB]. The phrase Χριστῷ τετηρημένοις 'Christ kept' is translated 'kept unharmed for Christ, kept unharmed through Christ' [BAGD]. The perfect tense indicates a continued state [BNTC, Hie, Hu, Law, TH, WBC] resulting from past action [Hie, Law, Lns, NIBC].

QUESTION—What relationship is indicated by the adjective κλητοῖς 'called', which is the last word in the verse?

It is governed by the definite article τοῖς 'the' at the beginning of the verse [AB, Alf, BNTC, EBC, EGT, El, Hie, ICC, Law, Lg, Lns, TH, WBC; all versions]: to the called ones.

1. It is modified by the two intervening participial phrases [Alf, EGT, El, Hie, ICC, Law, Lns, TH, WBC; ISV, NAB, NET, NIV, NJB, NLT, NRSV, REB, TEV]: to the called ones who are loved and kept.
2. It is translated as a parallel to the two participial phrases [AB; CEV, KJV, TNT] (but this would require καί 'and' to be added before κλητοῖς 'called'): to the ones who are chosen and loved and kept.

QUESTION—What relationship is indicated by ἐν 'in' in the phrase τοῖς ἐν θεῷ πατρὶ ἠγαπημένοις 'to the ones in God the Father loved'?

The absence of the definite article with both of these nouns puts emphasis on the nature of God the Father [Hie]. The phrase is variously understood, although the meaning comes out about the same. Some take it to mean that they are in God [Hie, ICC, Lns], in the intimate fellowship of God's love [WBC] and understand the phrase to mean that those who are in God the Father are loved by God [ICC; NRSV] or those who are in God the Father experience God's love [BNTC; NAB]. This places the emphasis on the relationship rather than on the agent of the participle 'loved' [Hie]. Others take it to mean they live in the love of God the Father [NET, NLT, REB, TEV]. Another view is that in regard to God the Father, they are loved by him [Alf]. Others take it to mean simply that they are loved by God the Father [EBC, NTC, TG; CEV, ISV, NJB, TNT].

QUESTION—What relationship is indicated by the two participles ἠγαπημένοις 'loved' and τετηρημένοις 'kept'?

They are attributive [El, Hie, Lns; ISV]: who are loved . . . and kept . . .

QUESTION—What relationship is indicated by the dative phrase Ἰησοῦ Χριστῷ 'Jesus Christ'?

1. It is an independent dative not governed by the preceding ἐν 'in' [AB, Alf, BNTC, El, Hie, Hu, Law, Lg(M), NIBC, TH, WBC; ISV, KJV, NET, NJB, NRSV, REB].
1.1 It indicates where the keeping takes place [KJV]: they are kept in Jesus Christ.
1.2 It indicates who does the keeping [AB; ISV]: they are kept by Jesus Christ.
1.3 It indicates the goal of the keeping [Alf, BNTC, El, Hie, Hu, Law, Lg(M), Lns, NIBC, TBST, WBC; NET, NJB, NRSV, REB]: they are kept for Jesus Christ by God the Father. It refers to keeping them for the

return of Jesus [Alf, BNTC, CBC, TBST, WBC; NET, REB]. It further implies the purpose of belonging to Jesus for eternity [Hu].
2. It is the second object of the preceding preposition ἐν 'in' [CEV, NAB, NIV, NLT, TEV]
 2.1 They are kept in Jesus Christ [NAB].
 2.2 They are kept by Jesus Christ [CEV, NIV, NLT, TEV]. They are loved by God and kept by Jesus [CEV, NIV]. They are called to live in the love of God and in the care of Jesus [NLT, TEV].

QUESTION—How is the participle τετηρημένοις 'kept' related in this clause?
 They are kept to be Christ's at his return [CBC, El, Hie, Hu, Lg(M), Lns, NIBC, TG, WBC].
 1. They are kept by God [BNTC, Hie, Hu, Law, Lns, NIBC, TBST, WBC].
 2. They are kept by Christ [CBC, EBC, TH, TNTC].

2 mercy to-you and peace and love be-multiplied.ᵃ

LEXICON—a. aorist pass. optative of πληθύνω (LN 59.68, 59.69) (BAGD 1.b. p. 669): 'to be multiplied' [AB, Alf, BAGD, BNTC, LN (59.68, 59.69), Lns; KJV], 'to be lavished' [NET], 'to be increased' [LN (59.69)]. This passive verb is also translated as an intransitive: 'to grow' [BAGD, LN (59.68)], 'to increase' [BAGD], 'to increase greatly' [LN (59.68)], 'to be (someone's) in abundance' [ISV, NIV, NJB, NRSV], 'to be (someone's) in full measure' [TEV], 'to be (someone's) in fullest measure' [REB], 'to be (someone's) in ever greater measure' [NAB], 'to be (someone's) abundantly' [TNT], 'to be given to (someone) in abundance' [WBC]. This verb is translated as present active: '(I pray that God) will greatly bless you with' [CEV], '(may you) receive more and more of' [NLT]. The optative mood expresses a wish [NTC], a hope [TH]. The singular form implies the bestowal of the three qualities as a unit [Hie]. This word implies that the believers already possess the qualities referred to [Hie]. The agent of the multiplying is God [El, NTC, WBC], as the passive voice implies [NTC].

QUESTION—What are the distinctions between 'mercy', 'peace', and 'love'?
 With variations, they form a common Christian greeting [CBC, EBC, TBST, TH]; they are three great characteristics of grace [Law, NIBC]. They proceed from God [Alf].
 1. 'Mercy' is God's behavior toward the 'called ones' [Hu], God's compassion [EBC, Hie, TH] shown through his action of salvation [BNTC, El, TH], God's attitude at the day of judgment and toward those who are in danger of straying spiritually [TBST], his loving concern [Law], love that pities and helps the needy [Hie, Lns], his kindness toward his people [WBC], help in the readers' dangerous situation [CBC, NIBC], the proper attitude of Christians toward those who have slipped away from true faith [TBST].
 2. 'Peace' is reconciliation with God [BNTC, Lns], a pure relationship with God [NIBC], confidence in Christ's work [EBC], confidence that God can

bring believers through dangers [TBST], calmness of mind and good conscience toward God [Hie, Law], the result of reconciliation to God [Hie], the result of a close relationship with God [TH, TNTC], the result of God's mercy [EGT, Hu, WBC].

3. 'Love' refers to God's love [BNTC, NIBC] through Christ [BNTC] to bring us to his presence in heaven [TBST], God's generous granting of his favor and meeting believers' needs [EBC]. It refers to the believers' love resulting from God's grace [Hu], a principle of heart and mind, based on God's love, that seeks the good of other persons [Hie]; it is brought to maturity in the realization of God's love [EGT]; it is based on the high value of each person in God's sight [Law].

DISCOURSE UNIT: 3–16 [GNT, TG; CEV, ISV, NIV, NLT, TEV]. The topic is false teachers [CEV, TEV], the danger of false teachers [ISV, NLT], the sin and doom of godless men [NIV], judgment on false teachers [GNT, TG].

DISCOURSE UNIT: 3–4 [AB, BNTC, EBC, EGT, Hie, Law, Lns, NTC, TBST, TNTC, WBC; NAB, NJB]. The topic is the reason for the letter [AB, EBC, EGT, Hie, Law, Lns, NTC, WBC; NJB] and its theme [WBC], the slipping in of deviants [AB], a threat to the faith [BNTC], churches in danger [TBST], an exhortation to be steadfast [NAB], the letter not written and the letter written [TNTC].

3 Beloved,[a] doing[b] all diligence/haste[c] to-write to-you concerning[d] our common[e] salvation,

TEXT—Some manuscripts omit ἡμῶν 'our'. GNT includes this word with an A decision, indicating that the text is certain. Only KJV omits 'our'.

LEXICON—a. ἀγαπητός (LN 25.45) (BAGD 2. p. 6): 'beloved' [AB, Alf, LN, Lns; KJV, NAB, NRSV], 'dearly loved friend' [NLT], 'dear friend' [BAGD, BNTC; CEV, ISV, NET, NIV, NJB, TNT], 'my dear friend' [WBC; TEV], 'my friend' [REB]. It implies that God's love has been put into their lives [EGT]; it refers to Jude's loving concern for his fellow Christians [El, Hie, Law, Lns, NIBC, NTC, TH] in spite of the unpleasant message he must give [Hie], because they were loved by God [Law, NIBC].

b. pres. mid. participle of ποιέω (LN 90.45) (BAGD II.1. p. 683): 'to do' [LN; TEV], 'to do for oneself' [BAGD], 'to do of oneself' [BAGD], 'to exercise' [Lns], 'to give' [Alf; KJV], not explicit [AB, BNTC, WBC; all versions except KJV, TEV]. The inclusion of πᾶσαν 'all' adds emphasis [Hu].

c. σπουδή (LN 25.74) (BAGD 2. p. 764): 'diligence' [Alf, Lns; KJV], 'eagerness, devotion' [LN]. The phrase πᾶσαν σπουδὴν ποιούμενος 'doing all diligence' is translated 'while eagerly preparing' [NRSV], 'at a time when I was eagerly looking forward' [NJB], 'although I was eager' [ISV], 'although I was very eager' [NIV], 'although I have been eager' [NET], 'although I am very eager' [WBC], 'I really wanted' [CEV], 'although I was making every effort' [BNTC], 'I was very much wanting' [TNT], 'I was already fully intent on' [NAB], 'I was fully intending' [REB], 'I was doing my best' [TEV], 'I had been eagerly planning' [NLT], 'be(ing) very eager' [BAGD], 'while making haste' [AB].

d. περί with genitive object (LN 89.6, 90.24): 'concerning' [Alf, LN (89.6, 90.24), Lns], 'about' [AB, BNTC, LN (90.24), WBC; all versions except KJV], 'in relation to, with regard to' [LN (89.6)], 'of' [LN (90.24); KJV].

e. κοινός (LN 57.9, **89.118**) (BAGD 1.a. p. 438): 'common' [AB, Alf, BAGD, BNTC, LN (57.9, **89.118**), Lns, WBC; KJV, NET], 'which we have in common' [LN (**89.118**)], 'communal' [BAGD], 'mutual, shared' [LN (57.9)]. The phrase τῆς κοινῆς ἡμῶν σωτηρίας 'our common salvation' is translated 'the salvation we share' [ISV, NAB, NIV, NRSV, REB], 'the salvation (which) we all share' [NJB, NLT, TNT], 'the salvation we share in common' [TEV], 'God's saving power at work in our lives' [CEV]. Κοινῆς 'common' here means that it was shared by all believers in this life [Alf, Blm, BNTC, EBC, El, Hie, Law, Lns, NIBC, TH], that it is open to everyone [TBST].

QUESTION—What is the function of this verse?

This and the following verse state the reason for writing this epistle [AB, BNTC, EBC, EGT, Hie, Hu, Law, Lns, NTC, WBC; NJB].

QUESTION—What relationship is indicated by the present participle in the phrase πᾶσαν σπουδὴν ποιούμενος 'doing all diligence'?

1. This means that he had been eager to write about salvation (but didn't—the participle indicating that the intention was not carried out), but instead wrote this exhortation [Hie, Law, Lg, NIBC, TG, WBC; CEV, ISV, NAB, NET, NJB, NLT, NRSV, REB, TNT]: I was eager to write about our common salvation, but instead I write this exhortation. This phrase implies the author's diligent intention [Hie]. The tense of the first infinitive 'to write' is present and seems to indicate a general intention that was not realized, while the tense of the second infinitive is aorist and points to an action that was carried through [BNTC].

2. This means that he was already eagerly writing (progressive participle) about salvation, but stopped to write this exhortation [Alf, EGT, ICC; TEV]: I was eagerly writing about our common salvation, but now write this exhortation. The present tense of the infinite implies action as well as wish [Alf].

3. This means that he was hurriedly writing about salvation, but changed to write this exhortation [AB]: I was hurriedly writing about our common salvation, but now write this exhortation.

QUESTION—What is the function of the participle ποιούμενος 'doing'?

The present tense implies action at the same time as the verb ἔσχον 'I had' [Alf, Hu], at the time of his occasion fro writing [Lg].

1. It is temporal [AB, Blm, El, Law, Lg; KJV, NJB, NRSV, REB, TEV, TNT]: while I was doing.

2. It is concessional [BNTC, NTC, WBC; ISV, NIV]: although I was doing.

3. It states a separate proposition in contrast with the following statement [CEV, NAB, NLT]: I was doing . . . , but . . .
QUESTION—What relationship is indicated by the present tense of the infinitive γράφειν 'to write'?
It refers to the general idea of writing [Alf]; it suggests less urgency [TH].
QUESTION—What relationship is indicated by σωτηρίας 'salvation'?
This phrase refers to the doctrines and practices related to salvation [Alf, Law, TH], to the fact of salvation [Law, TH], and the blessings involved [Hie]. It is possessed in this life [Alf, Blm, BNTC, EBC, Hu, Law, NIBC]. It will be completed only in the end time [TH]. It refers to final salvation in heaven [TBST, WBC].

I-had[a] (a) necessity[b] to-write to-you exhorting[c] to-contend[d] for-the faith[e] once-for-all[f] having-been-delivered[g] to-the saints.[h]

LEXICON—a. aorist act. indic. of ἔχω (LN 90.65): 'to have' [LN], 'to experience' [LN]. For the phrase ἀνάγκην ἔσχον 'I had a necessity', see b.

b. ἀνάγκη (LN 71.30) (BAGD 1. p. 52): 'necessity' [BAGD], 'obligation' [LN], 'necessary obligation' [LN], 'need' [TEV]. The phrase ἀνάγκην ἔσχον 'I had a necessity' is translated 'it was needful' [KJV], 'I find it necessary' [WBC; NRSV], 'I have found it necessary' [BNTC], 'I found it necessary' [AB, Alf; ISV], 'when I found it necessary' [REB], 'but now I feel obliged' [NAB], 'I was compelled' [Lns], 'I now feel compelled instead' [NET], 'when I felt the need' [TEV]; the phrase ἀνάγκην ἔσχον γράψαι 'I had a necessity to write' is translated 'But instead, I must write' [CEV], 'But now I find that I must write about something else' [NLT], 'I felt I had to write' [NIV], 'I felt that I must write' [NJB], 'when I felt that I had to write' [TNT]. It refers to necessity based on duty because of the entrance of the false teachers [Hu]. The urgency of the need to exhort them is greater that the need to write about the common salvation [NET].

c. pres. act. participle of παρακαλέω (LN 25.150, 33.168) (BAGD 2. p. 617): 'to exhort' [AB, Alf, BAGD; KJV], 'to urge' [BAGD, Lns; NIV, NLT, REB, TNT], 'to request, to ask for earnestly' [LN (33.168)], 'to ask' [CEV], 'to appeal to' [BAGD, LN (33.168), WBC; NRSV], 'to encourage' [BAGD, LN (25.150); NAB, NET, NJB, TEV]; this participle is translated as a phrase: 'with an appeal' [BNTC].

d. pres. pass. (deponent = act.) participle of ἐπαγωνίζομαι (LN **39.30**) (BAGD p. 281): 'to contend' [AB, BAGD, Lns; NIV, NRSV], 'to contend earnestly' [Alf; KJV, NET], 'to struggle for' [BNTC, LN], 'to join in the struggle for' [REB], 'to fight' [BAGD], 'to fight hard' [NAB, NJB], 'to fight on' [TEV], 'to carry on the fight for' [WBC], 'to defend' [CEV, NLT], 'to come to the defense of' [TNT], 'to continue (one's) vigorous defense' [ISV]. This is a strong word [BNTC]; it implies positive action, not merely defense [El, WBC], in spiritual, not physical, conflict [Hie], aiming to establish the true gospel [Hie]. The prefixed ἐπι- adds the idea of purpose to the verb [Alf, Hie]; it adds the idea of 'upon' [Law]; it strengthens the meaning of the verb [ICC, NTC]. The present tense implies that the struggle is to be continual [EBC, Hie, Law, NTC, TNTC].

e. πίστις (LN **31.104**) (BAGD 3. p. 664): 'faith' [AB, Alf, BNTC, **LN**, Lns, WBC; all versions except NLT], 'body of faith, body of belief' [BAGD], 'beliefs' [LN], 'doctrine' [BAGD, LN], 'truth of the Good News' [NLT]. It refers to the gospel [EGT, TG, WBC], the accepted Christian teachings [Alf, BNTC, CBC, EBC, EGT, El, Hie, Hu, ICC, Law, Lg, Lns, NIBC, NTC, TBST, TG, TH, TNTC, WBC; NET], or to Christianity as a movement [TH]. The definite article implies that this is the one true faith [Law]. The dative case here indicates the cause for which they should contend [BNTC, WBC].

f. ἅπαξ (LN **60.68**) (BAGD 2. p. 80): 'once for all' [Alf, BAGD, BNTC; CEV, NAB, NET, NIV, NLT, NRSV, REB], 'once and for all' [AB, **LN**, WBC; ISV, NJB, TEV, TNT], 'once and never again' [LN], 'once' [Lns; KJV]. It implies being finished [Hu], unalterable [BNTC, El, Lg, TBST, WBC], permanent [Lg], final [Hie, Lns], and normative [BNTC]. It adds emphasis to the particle παραδοθείσῃ 'having been handed over' [Law]. It is emphatic by word order [Law].

g. aorist pass. participle of παραδίδωμι (LN 33.237) (BAGD 3. p. 615): 'to be delivered' [AB, Alf, BNTC, Lns, WBC; KJV, NAB], 'to be handed down, to be passed on, to be transmitted' [BAGD], 'to be passed down' [ISV], 'to be entrusted' [NET, NIV, NJB, NRSV], 'to be instructed' [LN], 'to be taught' [BAGD, LN]. The participle παραδοθείσῃ 'having been delivered' is translated 'which God entrusted' [REB], 'that God has given' [CEV], 'which God has given' [TNT], 'God has given' [TEV], 'God gave' [NLT]. The implied immediate source is the apostles (and Christ [Hie]) [BNTC, Hie, Hu, Lg, NTC, TBST, TNTC, WBC]; the (ultimate [TBST, TNTC]) source is God [Law, TBST, TG, TNTC; CEV, NLT, REB, TEV, TNT] as the passive voice implies [Law]; the source is Christ [Lns, NIBC]. It indicates authoritative giving [BNTC, Hie]. The aorist tense implies prior action [Law], the fact of the transmission [Hie].

h. ἅγιος (LN 11.27, 88.24): 'holy' [LN (88.24)], 'saint' [AB, Alf, BNTC, Lns, WBC; ISV, KJV, NAB, NET, NIV, NRSV]. This plural noun is translated 'God's people' [LN (11.27); CEV, REB, TEV, TNT], 'God's holy people' [NJB, NLT]. It refers to all Christians [El, Hie, Hu, ICC, Lns, TBST, WBC], God's people in general [NIBC, TBST, TNTC], the members of the Christian Church [BNTC, NTC], the people whom God has set apart for himself [EBC, Lns], Christians who were consecrated to God [EGT, Hie, Lns, TG, TH] and called to be holy [EGT, Hie] as a duty [Hie], living a holy life [Lns].

QUESTION—What relationship is indicated by the aorist tense of the verb ἔσχον 'I had'?

1. It refers to an event prior to the time of writing [AB, Alf, Blm, BNTC, El, Hie, NIBC; NIV, NJB, REB, TEV, TNT]: I received a necessity to write

to you. The aorist tense refers to the event giving rise to the necessity [BNTC, El, Hie, Law].
2 It is epistolary, referring to the author's present feeling of necessity which will be in the past when the readers read the letter [Hie, Law, Lns, TG, WBC; NAB, NET, NLT, NRSV]: I now have a necessity to write to you. It implies prompt action [Hie]

QUESTION—What relationship is indicated by the aorist tense of the infinitive γράψαι 'to write'?

In contrast with the present tense of this verb in the preceding clause [Alf, BNTC, EGT, Law, Lns, NTC, TH], the aorist tense here refers to a specific occasion [Alf, BNTC, EGT, El, Hu, Law, NIBC, NTC, TNTC] which needed immediate attention [EGT, Law].
1. The urgent problem has replaced the intended general discussion [BNTC, EGT, El, Hie, Hu, ICC, Law, NIBC, NTC, TH, TNTC, WBC; CEV, NIV, NLT, REB, TEV, TNT].
2. This specific problem is included here together with the more general discussion [Alf, Blm], as a dominant part of the general discussion [TBST].

QUESTION—What relationship is indicated by the participle παρακαλῶν 'exhorting'?
1. It expresses purpose [TEV]: for the purpose of exhorting.
2. It indicates the type of writing the author intended [Hu].
3. It states an additional proposition [AB; CEV, ISV, KJV, NAB, NIV, NRSV, REB, TNT]: to write and exhort.

QUESTION—What is meant by the phrase ἅπαξ παραδοθείσῃ τοῖς ἁγίοις 'once for all having been delivered to the saints' modifying τῇ πίστει 'the faith'?

It describes the intrinsic nature of 'the faith' [Hie]. It implies that there are written documents such as letters from Paul and Peter and perhaps a gospel [NET]. God determined the contents of the Christian faith and it was to be taught without change [TG].

4 For certain/some[a] persons[b] have-crept-in,[c]

LEXICON—a. τις (LN 92.12): 'certain' [AB, Alf, BNTC, WBC; all versions except CEV, NLT, TEV], 'some' [Lns; CEV, ISV, NLT, TEV], 'someone' [LN].
  b. ἄνθρωπος (LN 9.1, 9.24): 'person' [BNTC, LN (9.1), WBC], 'individual' [NAB, REB, TNT], 'man' [AB, Alf, LN (9.24), Lns; KJV, NET, NIV], 'intruder' [NRSV]. This plural noun is translated 'people' [CEV, ISV, NJB, NLT, TEV]. Although it can be translated 'people', the false teachers were probably all men [NET].
  c. aorist act. indic. of παρεισδύω (LN **34.30**) (BAGD p. 624): 'to creep in' [AB, Alf], 'to creep in unawares' [KJV], 'to creep in covertly' [Lns], 'to slip in stealthily' [BAGD], 'to slip in unnoticed' [**LN**; ISV, TEV], 'to slip in secretly' [NIV], 'to slip in' [NET], 'to sneak in' [BAGD; CEV], 'to

worm one's way in' [NLT, REB], 'to worm one's way into' [NAB], 'to steal in' [NRSV], 'to infiltrate' [WBC; NJB], 'to join unnoticed' [LN], 'to make (one's) way in quietly' [TNT], 'to smuggle oneself in' [BNTC]. They entered the church in secrecy [Alf, Hie, Hu], without authorization [Hu], without a proper introduction [Alf], without having the characteristics of true believers [Hie]. They joined under false pretenses [TG]. They worked within the church and did not form a separate sect [BNTC, CBC, EBC, Law, Lg, NIBC, NTC, TNTC]. The aorist tense has the sense of the perfect tense [EGT, ICC, TH], implying that their past entrance has present effects [TH]; it refers to the situation which has occurred, causing the need for the letter [Alf, Law]. The prefixed preposition παρα- implies 'alongside' and the prefixed preposition εἰσ- implies 'into' [Law].

QUESTION—What relationship is indicated by γάρ 'for'?
1. It indicates the reason for writing this letter [Alf, EGT, Hu, ICC], why the author changed the content of his letter to the readers [Hie].
2. It indicates the reason for the need of contending for the faith [Blm, BNTC, EBC, ICC, Lg, Lns, NIBC, NTC, TBST, TH, TNTC].

QUESTION—What is implied by calling these people τινες ἄνθρωποι 'certain/some persons'?

It implies scorn [Alf, BNTC, NTC], or depreciation [El]. It implies that they are a minority [El, Hie] and divisive [Hie].
1. It refers to a specific but unnamed group [AB, Alf, BNTC, Law, Lg, NIBC, NTC, WBC; all versions except CEV, NLT, TEV]: certain persons (whose identity you know). They were probably itinerant teachers who intended to destroy the church [NTC].
2. It is indefinite [Hie, Hu, Lns; CEV, ISV, NLT, TEV]: some persons.

the-(ones) long-ago[a] written-beforehand[b] for[c] this judgment,[d]
LEXICON—a. πάλαι (LN 67.24) (BAGD 1., 2.a., p. 605): 'long ago' [BAGD (1), BNTC, LN, WBC; CEV, ISV, NAB, NET, NIV, NJB, NLT, NRSV, REB, TEV, TNT], 'ages ago' [AB], 'of old' [Alf; KJV], 'formerly' [BAGD (1)], 'a while back' [Lns], 'for a long time' [BAGD (2.a)]. This word emphasizes past time [El, NTC].
  b. perf. pass. participle of προγράφω (LN 33.66) (BAGD 1.b. p. 704): 'to be written beforehand' [LN], 'to be written about' [BAGD; ISV, NIV], 'to be written down in advance' [Lns], 'to be written down in prophecy' [Alf], 'to be marked out' [BAGD, BNTC; NET, TNT], 'to be marked down' [NJB], 'to be proscribed' [AB], 'to be destined' [NAB], 'to be designated' [WBC; NRSV], 'to be determined' [NLT], 'to be before ordained' [KJV]. It means being posted in writing previously [Law]. The phrase οἱ προγεγραμμένοι 'the ones written beforehand' is translated 'whom scripture marked down' [REB], 'the Scriptures predicted' [TEV], 'the Scriptures warned' [CEV]. The prefixed preposition προ- means 'before' in time [Alf, Hie, Hu]. It implies being foretold in writing [Hu,

TNTC], foretold and cited for trial and punishment [Blm]. The perfect tense indicates that the destiny of these persons was announced in writing in the past and is still applies to the present time [Hie, Law, Lns, NTC]. The passive voice implies the Holy Spirit as the actor [Law].
   c. εἰς with accusative object (LN 89.57, 90.23) (BAGD 4.d. p. 229): 'for' [AB, BAGD, BNTC, Lns, WBC; NAB, NET, NJB, NRSV, REB, TNT], 'for the purpose of' [LN (89.57)], 'to' [Alf; KJV], 'concerning' [LN (90.23)], 'as being deserving of' [ISV], not explicit [CEV, TEV].
   d. κρίμα (LN 56.24, 56.30) (BAGD 4.b. p. 450): 'judgment' [AB, Alf, LN (56.24)], 'fate' [NLT], 'verdict' [LN (56.24), Lns], 'sentence' [LN (56.24); REB], 'sentence of condemnation' [BAGD], 'condemnation' [BAGD, BNTC, LN (56.30), WBC; all versions except CEV, NLT, REB], 'punishment' [BAGD]. This noun is also translated as a verb: 'to be doomed' [CEV]. The suffix -μα indicates result [Lns]. The implication of condemnation is included [Hie], derived from the context [Alf, El, Hu].
QUESTION—To what does the phrase οἱ πάλαι προγεγραμμένοι 'the ones long ago written beforehand' refer?
   It was predicted by scripture [TEV], written in scripture [Law; REB], in OT books [Hie, Lg, TBST, TH, WBC], in previous prophecies [Alf, EBC, TNTC], in both OT and NT books [Law], in 2 Peter [Lns], in NT books already written [CBC, TBST], or in 1 Enoch [EGT, TBST], in the heavenly books in which God records each person's destiny [BNTC, NTC]. It implies being both described and destined [Alf], doomed for punishment as enemies of God [EGT], doomed for judgment because God foresaw their wickedness [Lg]. The definite article οἱ 'the ones' shows that this phrase is a further reference to the τινες ἄνθρωποι 'certain persons' [Alf, EGT]; the definite article emphasizes the character indicated by the participle [Lg]. The persons referred to are further described in verses 5–19 [WBC].
QUESTION—To what does the phrase τοῦτο τὸ κρίμα 'this judgment' refer?
   It refers to final doom [CEV] at Christ's coming [WBC]. It means condemnation [WBC; KJV, NIV], punishment [Lg(M)], that is described in the following verses [Hu, Lg, TH, TNTC, WBC; NAB, NET]. It is the condemnation 'on this account' [NJB, TNT]. It is the condemnation they have received [TEV] and are now enduring [REB] or the condemnation they will receive [TG], a sentence of judgment that is now impending [EGT]. It is a judgment in Jude's mind [Hie] but not specified [AB, Hie, ICC, NIBC]. It is fate [BNTC; NLT]. Τοῦτο 'this' refers to the fate to be described later [BNTC, El] in verses 5–18 [NET]; it refers to the comments in the rest of this verse [Lns]. It is probably the condemnation that Enoch prophesied (vv. 14–15) [TG]. The judgment comes from God [TNTC].

godless[a] (ones),
LEXICON—a. ἀσεβής (LN 53.11) (BAGD 1. p. 114): 'godless' [AB, BAGD, Lns; CEV, NAB, NIV, NLT, TEV, TNT], 'ungodly' [BNTC, LN, WBC; ISV, KJV, NET, NRSV], 'impious' [Alf], 'enemy of religion' [REB].

This word is translated 'without any reverence they . . . deny all religion' [NJB]. This word stands alone [Hu]. It implies total lack of reverence toward God [Hie, Law, NIBC], rejection of God's commands resulting in unrighteous behavior [WBC], sensuality [EGT]. It is the first of three descriptions of these persons in this verse [Law, NIBC]; this word is described by the two following phrases [Hu, Lg, TH]. It is a key word of the epistle [EGT, NIBC, TBST, WBC].

QUESTION—What relationship is indicated by this word?
1. It describes the τινες ἄνθρωποι 'certain persons' [AB, BNTC, Law; all versions except NJB, NRSV]: certain persons, (who are) godless ones.
2. It indicates the manner in which they change God's grace and deny Jesus [NJB]: they godlessly change . . . and deny . . .
3. It indicates how they were designated beforehand [WBC; NRSV]: designated beforehand as ungodly, for this condemnation.
4. It indicates why they deserved condemnation [ISV]: because they are ungodly.

changing^a the grace^b of-our God into^c licentiousness^d

LEXICON—a. pres. act. participle of μετατίθημι (LN **13.64**) (BAGD 2.a. p. 513): 'to change' [Alf, Lns; NIV], 'to turn' [LN; ISV, KJV, NET, TNT], 'to turn away from' [AB], 'to distort' [TEV], 'to pervert' [BAGD, BNTC, WBC; NAB, NJB, NRSV, REB]. This entire phrase is translated 'saying that God's forgiveness allows us to live immoral lives' [NLT], 'and are saying, "God treats us much better than we deserve, and so it is all right to be immoral"' [CEV]. It implies changing in a way which perverts the true meaning [Blm]. The present tense implies continuing action [Hie, Law, NTC].

b. χάρις (LN 25.89, 88.66) (BAGD 3.b. p. 878): 'grace' [Alf, BAGD, BNTC, LN (88.66), Lns, WBC; ISV, KJV, NET, NIV, NJB, NRSV], 'message about the grace' [TEV], 'gracious gift' [NAB], 'graciousness, kindness' [LN (88.66)], 'favor' [AB, BAGD, LN (25.89)], 'free favor' [REB], 'forgiveness' [NET], 'goodwill' [LN (25.89)], 'freedom' [TNT]. This noun is also translated as a verb phrase: 'to treat one better than he deserves' [CEV]. It refers to the state of salvation [Alf, BNTC], forgiveness [BNTC, Hie, Hu, WBC; NLT], and freedom from the Law [BNTC, Hu, WBC]. It is the gospel [ICC], God's forgiving love [NTC, TH] that is undeserved [TH], God's grace offered through Christ [Lg]. The phrase τὴν τοῦ θεοῦ ἡμῶν χάριτα 'the grace of our God' is emphatic by its position preceding the participle.

c. εἰς with accusative object (LN 13.62): 'into' [Alf, BNTC, Lns, WBC; ISV, KJV, NET, NIV, NRSV, REB, TNT], 'for' [LN], 'to' [AB; NAB, NJB], not explicit [CEV, NLT]. The phrase εἰς ἀσέλγειαν 'into licentiousness' is translated 'in order to excuse their immoral ways' [TEV]. This preposition expresses purpose [TH]; it introduces the word describing what God's grace has been changed into [Hu].

d. ἀσέλγεια (LN 88.272) (BAGD p. 114): 'licentiousness' [BAGD, BNTC; NRSV, REB], 'licentious behavior, licentious deeds, extreme immorality' [LN], 'license for evil' [NET], 'license for immorality' [NIV], 'immorality' [WBC], 'immoral way' [TEV], 'a source of immorality' [TNT], 'lasciviousness' [Alf; KJV], 'debauchery' [AB; NJB], 'uncontrollable lust' [ISV], 'sexual excess' [NAB], 'excess' [Lns], 'insolence' [BAGD]. This noun is also translated as a verb phrase: 'to be immoral' [CEV], 'to live an immoral life' [NLT]. It includes the full range of debauchery [Hie, TBST].

QUESTION—What is the function of this and the following phrase?

They state the two specific charges against the ἀσεβεῖς 'godless ones' [EBC, Hu, Lg; ISV].

QUESTION—What is the meaning of this phrase?

It means that they are promoting antinomianism [BNTC, Hie, Law], making the state of grace a license for immorality [Alf, Blm, EBC, Law, Lg, NTC, TNTC]; it means that these persons are living licentious lives [Lns, NIBC, NTC, TH].

QUESTION—How are the two nouns related in the genitive phrase τὴν τοῦ θεοῦ ἡμῶν χάριτα 'the grace of our God'?

The genitive noun θεοῦ 'God' is the source of χάριτι 'grace': the grace whose source is God. The inclusion of ἡμῶν 'our' emphasizes the sense of adoption [Lg], emphasizes the close relationship between Christians and God [Alf, TH] and between Christians, and thus emphasizes the abhorrence of those who misuse God's grace [Alf].

and denying[a] the only[b] Master[c] and our Lord Jesus Christ.

TEXT—Some manuscripts add θεόν 'God' after δεσπότην 'Master'. GNT rejects this addition with an A decision, indicating that the text is certain. Θεόν 'God' is added by KJV and by Blm in brackets.

LEXICON—a. pres. mid. (deponent = act.) of ἀρνέομαι (LN 34.48, 36.43) (BAGD 3.a. p. 108): 'to deny' [AB, Alf, BAGD, BNTC, LN (34.48), Lns, WBC; CEV, ISV, KJV, NAB, NET, NIV, NRSV], 'to repudiate' [BAGD], 'to disown' [BAGD; REB, TNT], 'to reject' [LN (36.43); NJB, TEV], 'to refuse to obey, to refuse to follow' [LN (36.43)], 'to turn against' [NLT]. The present tense implies continuing action [Lns, NTC]. The denial consisted in their wicked behavior [Hie, Hu, TNTC] and false beliefs [Hie]. They deny that they must obey Christ [CEV]. They deny the Second Coming and the Judgment [Lns].

b. μόνος (LN 58.50) (BAGD 1.a.δ. p. 527): 'only' [AB, Alf, BNTC, WBC; all versions], 'only one, one who alone is' [LN], 'only one who is' [BAGD], 'absolute' [Lns], not explicit [NET]. This makes a distinction between Christ and all false masters [ICC, Lns].

c. δεσπότης (LN 37.63) (BAGD p. 176): 'Master' [AB, Alf, BNTC, Lns, WBC; all versions except KJV, NAB, NIV], 'master' [BAGD, LN; NAB], 'ruler' [LN], 'lord' [BAGD, LN], 'Lord' [LN; KJV]. 'Sovereign' [NIV]. It implies absolute sovereignty [Law].

QUESTION—What relationship is indicated by the phrase τὸν μόνον δεσπότην καὶ κύριον ἡμῶν Ἰησοῦν Χριστόν 'the only Master and our Lord Jesus Christ'?

This phrase is emphatic, since it precedes the governing participle in word order in the Greek [Hie, Law]. The inclusion of ἡμῶν 'our' is emphatic [El].
1. Their immoral behavior is a denial of Christ's lordship [WBC].
2. It states what is denied [NIBC]: they deny that Jesus is their Master and Lord.

QUESTION—To whom does δεσπότην 'Master' refer?
1. If θεόν 'God' is not included in the text.
  1.1 It refers to Jesus [AB, Hie, ICC, Law, Lg, Lns, NTC, TBST, TH, WBC; all versions except KJV], because the definite article, τόν 'the', governs the entire phrase following it [Law, Lns, NTC; NET]: the only Master and our Lord, namely, Jesus Christ. Κύριον 'Lord' puts Jesus on the level of God [TH].
    1.1.1 Ἰησοῦν Χριστόν 'Jesus Christ' is in apposition with both δεσπότην 'Master' and κύριον 'Lord' [AB, Hie, ICC, Law, Lg, Lns, NTC, TBST, WBC; all versions except KJV]: our only Master and Lord, Jesus Christ. The pronoun ἡμῶν 'our' modifies both δεσπότην 'Master' and κύριον 'Lord' [Law, Lns].
    1.1.2 Ἰησοῦν Χριστόν 'Jesus Christ' is in apposition with only κύριον 'Lord': the only Master (i.e., Jesus) and our Lord Jesus Christ.
  1.2 It refers to God the Father [Alf, BNTC, CBC, EBC, EGT, Hu, NIBC, TNTC]: the only Master (God), and our Lord Jesus Christ. This meaning is strengthened by μόνον 'only' [Alf, BNTC, EBC, EGT, TNTC].
2. If θεόν 'God' is included.
  2.1 It refers to God the Father [KJV]: the only Master, namely, God, and our Lord Jesus Christ.
  2.2 It refers to Jesus [Blm]: our only Master God, namely, Jesus Christ.

DISCOURSE UNIT: 5–19 [NAB]. The topic is comments against false teachers.

DISCOURSE UNIT: 5–16 [EBC]. The topic is a warning against false teachers.

DISCOURSE UNIT: 5–15 [Lg]. The topic is examples of God's justice and description of the character and the sins of the deceivers.

DISCOURSE UNIT: 5–13 [EGT]. The topic is illustrations of sin and judgment, from history and from nature.

DISCOURSE UNIT: 5–11 [CBC]. The topic is judgments by God.

DISCOURSE UNIT: 5–10 [Lns, WBC]. The topic is three examples of judgment and their application [Lns], three OT types [WBC].

DISCOURSE UNIT: 5–8 [TBST]. The topic is a warning by three examples of OT judgment.

DISCOURSE UNIT: 5–7 [AB, BNTC, EBC, Hie, Law, NTC, TNTC; NJB]. The topic is three notorious examples [BNTC], three OT examples of crimes judged [AB], three warning reminders [TNTC], examples from history [NTC], examples of God's judgment in history [EBC], accounts of past apostasy [Law], the historical fate of apostates [Hie], the certainty of punishment of the false teachers [NJB].

5 But/Now I-desire^a to-remind you,

LEXICON—a. pres. mid. (deponent = act.) of βούλομαι (LN 25.3, 30.56) (BAGD 2.a.δ. p. 146): 'to desire' [LN (25.3); NET, NRSV], 'to wish' [Alf; NAB], 'to want' [AB, BAGD, LN (25.3); ISV, NIV, TEV, TNT], 'to like' [BNTC, WBC; NJB], 'to purpose, to plan' [LN (30.56)], 'to intend' [LN (30.56)], 'to will' [KJV], 'to be the intent (of someone)' [Lns]. This entire phrase is translated 'I must remind you' [NLT], 'but let me remind you' [REB], 'don't forget what happened' [CEV]. It implies a wish based on deliberation [Hie].

QUESTION—What relationship is indicated by δέ 'but'?
  1. It indicates a transition [Hu, Law, Lns; ISV, NET, NRSV] to something additional but different [Hie].
  2. It indicates a contrast [Alf, ICC, Lg(M)] with the impiety of the persons just mentioned [El].

QUESTION—What is the function of this clause and the following participial phrase, 'I desire to remind you, you knowing all things'?
  These phrases relate to verses 5–7 [TH]. The aorist tense of the infinitive ὑπομνῆσαι 'to remind' points to the historical event the author will mention [Law].
  1. It is merely a reminder, since the readers knew the OT stories [El, Lns, NTC, WBC] and the apostolic teaching [WBC]. It is an expression of courtesy, avoiding the implication that the readers were ignorant of the situation [AB, Hie, NTC]. It is an apology for recalling things they already know well [BNTC, TH] or a polite form [TH]. It refers to previous apostolic teaching [NTC, TNTC].
  2. The author is not really reminding them, since he deals with things they did not know [ICC].

you knowing^a all-things,^b that the Lord once^c having-saved^d a-people^e out-of^f (the) land^g of-Egypt,

TEXT—Instead of εἰδότας ... πάντα ὅτι ὁ κύριος ἅπαξ 'knowing all things, that the Lord once', some manuscripts read εἰδότας ... ἅπαξ πάντα (or τοῦτο), ὅτι ὁ κύριος 'knowing once all things (or this), that the Lord'. GNT accepts the former reading with a D decision, indicating that the Committee had great difficulty in arriving at a decision. The former text is read by EBC, EGT, Lns, TH, ISV, NRSV, REB, TEV. The latter text, with πάντα 'all things', is read by Alf, BNTC, El, Hie, ICC, Hu, Law, Lg, TNTC, WBC, and TNT; with τοῦτο 'this', by Blm and KJV; with uncertainty concerning whether they read πάντα 'all things' or τοῦτο 'this' by AB, NTC, TBST, NAB, NIV, NJB, and NLT. It is uncertain whether CEV follows the former or the latter text.

TEXT—Instead of ὁ κύριος 'the Lord', some manuscripts read Ἰησοῦς 'Jesus', and some manuscripts read θεός 'God'. GNT includes this variant with the preceding one and reads [ὁ] κύριος 'the Lord' with a D decision, indicating that the Committee had great difficulty in arriving at a decision. Ἰησοῦς 'Jesus' is read by AB, Alf, CBC, El, NET; θεός 'God' is read by none.

LEXICON—a. perf. (with pres. meaning) act. participle of οἶδα (LN 28.1, 29.6, 32.4): 'to know' [AB, Alf, LN (28.1), Lns; KJV, NIV, NLT, REB, TEV, TNT], 'to be aware of' [NAB], 'to be fully aware of' [ISV], 'to be informed' [BNTC, WBC; NET, NRSV], 'to understand, to comprehend' [LN (32.4)], 'to remember, to recall, to recollect' [LN (29.6)], 'to learn' [NJB]. The perfect tense with present meaning refers to knowing at the time of this writing [Hie, Lg(M)]. The readers knew the stories but did not understand them [TBST].

b. πᾶς (LN 59.23): 'all' [LN; TNT], 'every' [LN]; as a plural: 'everything' [Lns], 'all things' [Alf, BNTC, WBC], 'all this' [REB, TEV], 'all about this' [AB], 'these things' [ISV], 'certain things' [NAB], 'it' [NLT]; uncertain [NIV, NJB]; different text [KJV]. The phrase εἰδότας ὑμᾶς πάντα 'you knowing all things' is translated 'though you are fully informed' [NET, NRSV]. It refers to all things related to the topic [Alf, Hie, Hu], all that follows [EGT, El, TBST], all the OT story of deliverance from Egypt [Law], all the essentials of the apostolic faith [WBC].

c. ἅπαξ (LN 60.67, 60.68, 60.69) (BAGD 2. p. 80): 'once, one time' [LN (60.67)], 'once and never again' [LN (60.68)], 'once and for all' [LN (60.69)], 'once for all' [BAGD; NET]; for those who read this word following κύριος 'Lord': 'once' [Lns; ISV, TEV], 'once for all' [NRSV, REB]; for those who read this word following εἰδότας 'knowing': 'already' [NAB, NIV, TNT], 'once' [AB; KJV], 'once for all' [BNTC], 'once and for all' [WBC; NJB], 'well' [NLT], 'already' [TNT], 'as you do' [Alf].

d. aorist act. participle of σῴζω (LN 21.18) (BAGD 1.b. p. 798): 'to save' [AB, Alf, BNTC, Lns, WBC; ISV, KJV, NET, NRSV, TNT], 'to deliver' [LN; NIV, REB], 'to rescue' [LN; CEV, NAB, NJB, NLT, TEV], 'to bring out safely' [BAGD]. Here it implies more than mere physical deliverance [Hie].

e. λαός (LN 11.12, 11.55) (BAGD 3.a. p. 466): 'people' [AB, BAGD, LN (11.55), Lns, WBC; NRSV], 'the people' [Alf; KJV, NET, TNT], 'those people' [CEV], 'the people of Israel' [TEV], 'his people' [BNTC; ISV, NAB, NIV, REB], 'people of God' [LN (11.12)], 'nation' [LN (11.55)], 'the nation' [NJB], 'the whole nation of Israel' [NLT]. This word is

emphatic by forefronting [Alf, Hie], and may thus imply 'the people' even without the definite article [Alf]. Without the definite article it refers to Israel as an entire people [Hie, Hu, Law]; it has qualitative force, emphasizing the concept of 'people' [Lns].
  f. ἐκ with genitive object (LN 84.4) (BAGD 1.a. p. 234): 'out of' [Alf, BAGD, BNTC, LN, Lns, WBC; KJV, NET, NIV, NRSV, REB, TNT], 'out from' [LN], 'away from' [BAGD], 'from' [AB, BAGD, LN; CEV, ISV, NAB, NJB, NLT, TEV].
  g. γῆ (LN 1.79): 'land' [AB, Alf, BNTC, LN, WBC; ISV, KJV, NAB, NET, NRSV]. The phrase γῆς Αἰγύπτου 'land of Egypt' is translated 'Egypt' [Lns; NIV, NJB, NLT, REB, TEV, TNT].
QUESTION—What is indicated by ὑμᾶς 'you' in this phrase?
  Its presence and position adds emphasis [Lg(M)], contrast with the false teachers [Hie]: to remind you, you who know . . .
QUESTION—What relationship is indicated by the participle εἰδότας 'knowing'?
  1. It expresses a concession [Hie, ICC, NTC, WBC; ISV, KJV, NAB, NET, NIV, NJB, NRSV, TEV]: although you know.
  2. It expresses cause [EGT, Hu, Lns]: because you know. This word justifies the author's comment that he is reminding them [EGT].
  3. It expresses reinforcement [BNTC; NLT, TNT]: and you know it.
  4. It is translated as an independent statement in contrast with the preceding statement [AB; REB]: you know . . . but let me remind you.
QUESTION—What is the clause introduced by ὅτι 'that' connected with?
  It is connected with ὑπομνῆσαι 'to remind' [El, Hu]: to remind you that . . .
QUESTION—What is ἅπαξ 'once' connected with?
  1. If this word is read following κύριος 'Lord', it is connected with σώσας 'having saved' [EBC, Lns, TH; ISV, NRSV, REB, TEV]: the Lord once having saved.
  2. If this word is read following εἰδότας ὑμας 'you knowing'.
  2.1 It is connected with εἰδότας 'knowing' [AB, Alf, BNTC, El, Hie, Hu, ICC, Law, Lg, NIBC, NTC, TBST, TNTC; KJV, NAB, NET, NIV, NJB, NLT, TNT]: you knowing all things once for all. It emphasizes that a new teaching is not needed [Hu]. They had learned it from reading 2 Peter, where the same illustrations are given [NET].
  2.2 It is connected with ὑπομνῆσαι 'to remind' [Blm]: I wish to remind you once more.
QUESTION—To whom does κύριος 'Lord' refer?
  1. It refers to God [BNTC, EBC, Hie, Hu, Law, NIBC, NTC, TBST, TH, TNTC]: God having saved a people.
  2. It refers to Christ [ICC]: Christ having saved a people.
QUESTION—What relationship is indicated by the participle σώσας 'having saved'?
  The aorist tense indicates action prior to the following verb ἀπώλεσεν 'he destroyed' [Alf].

1. It is a concession [AB; NLT]: even though the Lord had saved . . .
2. It is temporal [BNTC, Lns]: after the Lord had saved . . .
3. It is attributive [WBC; ISV, NRSV, TNT]: the Lord who saved . . .
4. It is translated as an independent statement in contrast with the following statement [NAB, NIV, NJB, TEV]: the Lord rescued . . . , but he destroyed . . .

the second-time[a] the-(ones) not having-believed[b] he-destroyed,[c]

LEXICON—a. δεύτερος (LN 60.49, **67.50**) (BAGD 4. p. 177): 'second time' [BAGD, Lns], 'second occasion' [WBC], 'second' [LN (60.49)], 'next time' [BNTC], 'afterward' [AB, LN (67.50); KJV, NJB, NRSV, TEV], 'later' [CEV, ISV, NAB, NET, NIV, NLT, REB, TNT]. This word is also translated as an adverb: 'secondly' [Alf].

b. aorist act. participle of πιστεύω (LN 31.85) (BAGD 1.d. p. 661): 'to believe' [Alf, BAGD, BNTC, LN, Lns, WBC; ISV, KJV, NET, NIV, NRSV, REB, TEV, TNT], 'to have faith' [CEV]. The participial phrase τοὺς μὴ πιστεύσαντες 'the ones not having believed' is translated 'those who refused to believe' [NAB], 'the people who refused to believe him' [NJB], 'those who were unfaithful' [AB], 'everyone of those who did not remain faithful' [NLT]. This participial phrase refers to lack of faith in Moses' power and God's promises [BNTC], unbelief resulting in disobedience (rebellion [EBC]) [Blm, EBC, TH, WBC], rejection of God's power and provision [Law], rejection of God's leadership [NTC], lack of faithfulness [AB]. The aorist tense implies a positive action [Law]. It refers to the unbelief and rebellion at Kadesh-Barnea in unwillingness to enter the Promised Land [Hie].

c. aorist act. indic. of ἀπόλλυμι (LN 20.31) (BAGD 1.a.α. p. 95): 'to destroy' [AB, Alf, BAGD, BNTC, Law, LN, Lns, WBC; all versions]. They were destroyed by God letting them perish in the wilderness [Law, Lns, NIBC, NTC, TBST], by being destroyed in the wilderness [Alf, BNTC, Hie] and being denied entrance into the Promised Land [Alf, NIBC]. The aorist tense summarizes the destruction through the following forty years [Hie]. It implies that God will deal similarly with the false teachers [Blm].

QUESTION—To what does τὸ δεύτερον 'the second time' refer?
1. It refers to a second act [Alf, El, Hie, Hu], the destruction of unbelievers [AB, BNTC; all versions except NJB] in the wilderness [Alf, EBC, EGT, El, Hie, Hu, ICC, Law, Lg(M), Lns, NTC, TNTC, WBC], the first act being the deliverance from Egypt [AB, Alf, BNTC, EBC, EGT, Hie, Hu, Law, Lg(M), Lns; all versions except ISV, NJB].
2. It refers to the Babylonian captivity as 'the second act', the first being the judgment which caused the unbelievers to perish in the wilderness [Lg].

QUESTION—What relationship is indicated by the forefronted position of the participial phrase τοὺς μὴ πιστεύσαντας 'the ones not having believed'?
It implies that they are a distinct group [Hie].

6 and angels the-(ones) not having-kept[a] their-own domain[b]
LEXICON—a. aorist act. participle of τηρέω (LN 13.32) (BAGD 3. p. 815): 'to keep' [Alf, BAGD, BNTC, LN, Lns, WBC; ISV, KJV, NIV, NRSV], 'to keep to' [AB; NAB, NJB, TNT], 'to keep within' [NET], 'to stay within' [NLT, TEV], 'to retain' [LN], 'to be content to maintain' [REB]. This entire phrase is translated 'You also know about the angels who didn't do their work' [CEV]. The aorist tense refers to a completed prior act [Law, Lns, NIBC, NTC]. This attributive participle is interpreted as implying a reason, 'because they did not keep' [El].
  b. ἀρχή (LN **37.55**) (BAGD 4. p. 112): 'domain' [BAGD; NAB, NET, TNT], 'dominion' [BNTC; REB], 'principality' [Lns], 'sphere of influence' [BAGD], 'sphere of (one's) rule' [**LN**], 'limit of (one's) rule' [LN], 'authority' [NJB], 'limits of (one's) authority' [TEV], 'sphere of authority' [LN], 'position of authority' [WBC], 'position' [AB; ISV, NRSV], 'dignity' [Alf], 'first estate' [KJV]. This singular noun is translated as a plural: 'positions of authority' [NIV], 'limits of authority' [NLT]. It refers to office and dignity [EGT, Law, NIBC], stipulated responsibilities [EBC, TBST], authority [TG, TH], rule [Law], government or province [ICC], power [WBC] or dominion [Hu, WBC], power over earthly things [El], domain [Law], exalted position [Hie, NTC], the bounds determined by God [NET]. They deserted their place of authority appointed by God to go after a position that was not intended for them [NIBC].
QUESTION—What relationship is indicated by τε 'and'?
  It indicates a close connection with the preceding comment [Alf, Hie, Hu, Lns, NTC]. This continues the sentence which starts in verse 5, but due to its length can be started anew: 'You also know that/about . . .' [CEV, NET].
QUESTION—What is indicated by ἀγγέλους 'angels' without a definite article?
  The angels referred to are identified by the following articular participial phrase τοὺς μὴ τηρήσαντας . . . 'the ones not having kept . . .' [AB, Alf, Hie, Hu, ICC, Lg(M), Lns; NAB].
  1. 'Angels' without the article is indefinite [Hu; NAB]: angels. It refers to angels generally [Hu].
  2. 'Angels' without the article is qualitative [Hie, Law, Lg(M), Lns], emphasizing their high position [Hie, Law, Lns], contrasting them with mankind [Lg(M)]: (beings no less than) angels.
  3. 'Angels' is treated as definite [BNTC; all versions except NAB]: the angels.

but having-deserted[a] their-own dwelling,[b]
LEXICON—a. aorist act. participle of ἀπολείπω (LN **15.59**) (BAGD 3. p. 94): 'to desert' [BAGD, **LN**; NAB], 'to abandon' [BNTC, LN, Lns, WBC; ISV, NET, NIV, REB, TEV], 'to leave' [AB, Alf, LN; CEV, KJV, NJB, NLT, NRSV, TNT]. It implies deliberate abandonment [Hie]. The aorist

tense indicates a definite completed prior act [Law, Lns, NIBC]. This participial phrase together with the preceding participial phrase, τοὺς μὴ τηρήσαντας 'the ones not having kept', emphasizes the apostasy of these angels [WBC].

 b. οἰκητήριον (LN **85.68**) (BAGD 1. p. 557): 'dwelling' [BAGD; NRSV], 'dwelling place' [BNTC, **LN**; NAB, REB, TEV], 'habitation' [Alf, Lns; KJV], 'abode' [AB], 'home' [LN, WBC; NIV, TNT], 'assigned place' [ISV], 'place of residence' [NET], 'appointed sphere' [NJB]. The phrase τὸ ἴδιον οἰκητήριον 'their own dwelling' is translated 'the place where they belonged' [NLT]. This singular noun is translated as a plural: 'proper places' [CEV]. It refers to heaven [Alf, BNTC, CBC, El, Hie, Hu, ICC, NIBC, NTC, TG], the very presence of God [CBC, Law, Lns, TH], their assigned dwelling of light [Lg]. It is 'their own' because God assigned it to them [ICC, NTC; NET].

QUESTION—What relationship is indicated by ἀλλά 'but'?

It indicates a strong contrast with the preceding statement [Hie]. It strengthens (explains [Hu]) the preceding negative phrase [Hu, NTC]; it states the positive aspect of the same action which is described negatively in the preceding participial phrase [Hie].

QUESTION—To what does this phrase refer?

 1. It refers to the incident referred to in Genesis 6:1–4, taking the interpretation that the 'sons of God' are fallen angels [Alf, BNTC, CBC, Hie, ICC, Law, NIBC, TBST, TNTC, WBC].

 2. It does not refer to Genesis 6:1–4, since angels do not have physical bodies [NTC].

for[a] judgment of-(the)-great[b] day in-eternal[c] chains[d] under[e] gloom[f] he-has-kept,[g]

LEXICON—a. εἰς with accusative object (LN 89.57, 67.117, 67.119): 'for' [AB, LN (67.117), Lns; ISV, NET, NIV, NLT, NRSV, REB, TEV], 'for the purpose of' [LN (89.17)], 'until' [LN (67.119), WBC; CEV, NJB], 'to' [LN (67.119)], 'unto' [KJV], 'awaiting' [BNTC], 'against' [Alf; NAB].

 b. μέγας (LN 78.2, 87.22) (BAGD 2.b.β. p. 498): 'great' [AB, Alf, BAGD, BNTC, LN (78.2, 87.22), Lns, WBC; all versions except NLT], 'important' [BAGD, LN (87.22)], 'terrible' [LN (78.2)]. The phrase κρίσιν μεγάλης ἡμέρας 'judgment of the great day' is translated 'the great day of Judgment' [CEV], 'the day of judgment' [NLT], 'that great Day on which they will be condemned' [TEV].

 c. ἀΐδιος (LN 67.96) (BAGD p. 22): 'eternal' [Alf, BAGD, BNTC, LN, WBC; ISV, NET, NJB, NRSV, TEV], 'everlasting' [AB, Lns; CEV, KJV, NIV, REB, TNT], 'perpetual' [NAB]. The phrase δεσμοῖς ἀϊδίοις ὑπὸ ζόφον 'in eternal chains under gloom' is translated 'chained in prisons of darkness' [NLT]. This word implies being escape-proof [Hie, Law], unbreakable [Hu], eternal and unchangeable [NIBC]. Although referred to

as 'eternal', these chains are for use only until the final judgment [EGT, WBC].
d. δεσμός (LN 6.14) (BAGD 1. p. 176): 'chain' [AB, BNTC, LN, WBC; all versions except NAB, NJB, NLT], 'fetter' [BAGD, LN], 'bond' [Alf, BAGD, LN, Lns; NJB], 'bondage' [NAB].
e. ὑπό with accusative object (LN 83.51) (BAGD 2.a.β. p. 843): 'under' [Alf, BAGD, BNTC, LN, Lns; KJV], 'in' [AB, WBC; all versions except KJV, NAB, NLT], 'shrouded in' [NAB]. The use of this preposition implies that the gloom covers these angels [Hu], is brooding over them [Alf, Hie].
f. ζόφος (LN 14.57) (BAGD 2. p. 339): 'gloom' [BAGD, LN], 'darkness' [AB, Alf, BAGD, BNTC, LN; KJV, NET, NIV, NJB, NLT, REB, TNT], 'deepest darkness' [ISV, NRSV], 'murky darkness' [NAB], 'nether darkness' [WBC], 'darkness below' [TEV], 'blackness' [Lns], 'dark pit' [CEV]. It implies the misery of the condition [NIBC]. It refers to the second heaven of late Jewish and early Christian thinking [BNTC]; it refers to the world of the dead [TH].
g. perf. act. indic. of τηρέω (LN 37.122) (BAGD 2.a. p. 815): 'to keep' [AB, Alf, BAGD, BNTC, Lns, WBC; all versions except ISV, KJV, REB], 'to hold' [BAGD; REB], 'to reserve' [KJV], 'to guard' [LN]; this active voice is translated as a passive: 'to be held' [ISV]. It is emphatic by its final position [Hie]. The implied subject is God [EBC; CEV, NLT, REB, TEV], the Lord [BNTC; NAB]. The perfect tense implies a past action which is still in effect [Hie, Hu, Law, NIBC, NTC]. This word here is in sharp (ironical [NIBC, TH, WBC]) contrast with (opposition to [Lg(M)]) the same word in participial form, μὴ τηρήσαντας 'not having kept' at the beginning of this verse with regard to the fallen angels [Alf, El, Lg(M), NIBC, TH, WBC; NET].

QUESTION—How are the two nouns related in the genitive construction κρίσιν μεγάλης ἡμέρας 'judgment of the great day'?

'Great day' states when the judgment will occur [NIBC; ISV, NIV, REB, TEV, TNT]: judgment on the great day. It refers to the final judgment [EBC, EGT, Hie, Hu, Law, NIBC, TH] with penalty [Law], to punishment [Hu], to condemnation [TEV], at the end of the world [Alf, Lg, TH], at Christ's return [Lns].

7 as Sodom and Gomorrah and the cities around[a] them (in) the similar[b] manner[c] to-these having-committed-sexual-immorality[d] and having-gone-out[e] after[f] different[g] flesh,[h]

LEXICON—a. περί with accusative object (LN **83.18**) (BAGD 2.a.γ. p. 645): 'around' [AB, LN], 'about' [Alf; KJV], 'near' [BAGD, Lns; ISV], 'nearby' [CEV, TEV], 'neighboring' [WBC; NJB, NLT, REB, TNT], 'surrounding' [BNTC; NET, NIV, NRSV], 'thereabout' [NAB].
b. ὅμοιος (LN 64.1) (BAGD 1. p. 566): 'similar' [Lns; NET, NIV], 'like' [Alf, LN; KJV], 'same' [BAGD, BNTC, WBC; NJB, NRSV], not explicit

[CEV]. The phrase τὸν ὅμοιον τρόπον τούτοις 'the similar manner to these' is translated 'likewise' [AB], 'like them' [ISV], 'like the angels' [REB], 'they too' [TNT], 'whose people acted as those angels did' [TEV], not explicit [NLT].

c. τρόπος (LN 89.83) (BAGD 1. p. 827): 'manner' [Alf, LN, Lns; KJV, NRSV], 'way' [BAGD, BNTC, LN, WBC; NET, NIV], not explicit [CEV]. The phrase τὸν ὅμοιον τρόπον 'the similar manner' is translated 'just as' [BAGD; NAB].

d. aorist act. participle of ἐκπορνεύω (LN **88.271**) (BAGD p. 244): 'to commit sexual immorality' [**LN**], 'to give oneself up to sexual immorality' [NIV], 'to be filled with sexual immorality' [NLT], 'to indulge in sexual immorality' [NET, NRSV, TEV], 'to indulge in immorality' [BAGD], 'to practice immorality' [BNTC, WBC], 'to give oneself over to fornication' [KJV], 'to follow fornication' [Alf], 'to commit fornication' [AB, LN; REB], 'to commit exceeding fornication' [Lns], 'to commit sexual sins' [ISV], 'to engage in illicit sex' [LN], 'to become immoral' [CEV], 'to indulge in lust' [NAB]. The phrase ἐκπορνεύσασαι καὶ ἀπελθοῦσαι ὀπίσω σαρκὸς ἑτέρας 'having committed sexual immorality and having gone out after different flesh' is translated 'indulged in unrestricted and unnatural sexual vice' [TNT]. The prefixed preposition ἐκ- is intensive [Hie, Hu, Law, Lg, Lns]; it implies action without reserve [Alf, Hie, Lg].

e. aorist act. participle of ἀπέρχομαι (LN 15.37, **88.279**) (BAGD 4. p. 84): 'to go' [AB, BAGD; KJV], 'to go away' [Alf, LN (15.37), Lns], 'to leave' [LN (15.37)], 'to hanker' [WBC], 'to lust' [BNTC]. The phrase 'to go after' is translated 'to do' [CEV], 'to engage in' [ISV], 'to practice' [NAB], 'to indulge in' [REB], 'to pursue' [NET, NJB, NRSV]. Some combine this verb with the preceding verb 'to commit sexual immorality' [Hie; NET, NIV, TEV, TNT]. This word implies leaving normal actions for unnatural ones [Alf, Hie]. The prefixed ἀπο- implies turning away from [Hu].

f. ὀπίσω (LN 36.35) (BAGD 2.a.β. p. 575): 'after' [AB, Alf, BAGD, BNTC, LN, Lns, WBC; KJV].

g. ἕτερος (LN 58.36): 'different' [BNTC, LN], 'strange' [WBC; KJV], 'other' [AB, Alf, Lns], 'all sorts of' [CEV], 'every kind of' [NLT], 'unnatural' [NAB, NET, NJB, NRSV, REB, TNT]. (For the phrase 'different flesh' see h. for ISV, NIV, TEV.) Here ἕτερος means different in kind [NIBC], in quality and character [Law], beyond what is natural [Alf, EGT, El, Hie, Law, Lg, TNTC, WBC], perversion of the created order [NTC].

h. σάρξ (LN 88.279) (BAGD 1. p. 743): 'flesh' [BAGD, BNTC; KJV], 'lust' [NRSV], 'lusts' [NJB, REB], 'sexual vice' [TNT], 'sexual sins' [CEV], 'sexual perversion' [NLT], 'desire' [NET]. The phrase 'different flesh' is translated 'perversion' [NIV, TEV], 'homosexual activities' [ISV], 'homosexual intercourse' [LN (88.279)].

QUESTION—What relationship is indicated by ὡς 'as'?
1. It introduces a similar example [AB, BNTC, Hie, Hu, WBC; ISV, KJV, NRSV]: likewise . . .
2. It introduces an additional example [Alf, Lg, Lns, NTC; CEV, NAB, NIV, NJB, REB, TEV, TNT]: in addition . . .

QUESTION—To what does the phrase Σόδομα καὶ Γόμορρα καὶ αἱ περὶ αὐτὰς πόλεις 'Sodom and Gomorrah and the cities around them' refer?
It refers to the inhabitants of those cities [Blm, Hu, WBC].

QUESTION—What is the phrase τὸν ὅμοιον τρόπον τούτοις 'the similar manner to these' connected with?
It implies a close connection with the preceding verse [Hu], with the angels in verse 6 [TH, WBC], with verses 5–6 [Lns]. The similarity lies in the eternal penalty of all those mentioned [Lns].
1. It is connected with the two following participles [Alf, BNTC, El, Lg(M), Lns, WBC; all versions except CEV, KJV, NLT]: having committed . . . and having gone out . . . in a similar manner to these.
2. It is connected with the preceding phrase αἱ περὶ αὐτὰς πόλεις 'the cities around them' [KJV]: the cities around them in a similar manner.

QUESTION—To what does τούτοις 'these' refer?
1. It refers to (the men of [Lg, NTC]) Sodom and Gomorrah [Lg, NTC]: in a similar manner to (the men of) these cities.
2. It refers to the angels mentioned in verse 6 [Alf, BNTC, EBC, EGT, El, Hie, Hu, ICC, Law, TG, WBC; NAB, REB, TEV]: in a similar manner to those angels.
3. It refers both to the angels previously mentioned and to the Israelites who were destroyed in the wilderness [Lns]: in a similar manner to those persons and angels.
4. It refers to the false teachers mentioned in verse 4 [Lg(M)]: in a manner similar to those false teachers.

QUESTION—What relationship is indicated by the two participles ἐκπορνεύσασαι 'having committed sexual immorality' and ἀπελθοῦσαι 'having gone out'?
They explain what the sins of Sodom and Gomorrah were [Hie]. The aorist tenses indicate the past actions [Law, Lns]. They are connected with the cities mentioned earlier in the verse [Lns]. Ἀπελθοῦσαι 'having gone out' intensifies the sense of the preceding participle [Lns]; it explains the first participle [WBC].
1. They are treated as attributive participles [BNTC; ISV, NLT, NRSV]: which committed . . . and went out after . . .
2. They are translated as causal [Lns]: because they committed . . . and went out after . . .
3. They are translated as independent actions [AB; CEV, NAB, NIV, REB, TEV, TNT]: they committed sexual immorality and did all sorts of sexual sins.

QUESTION—What meant by ἀπελθοῦσαι ὀπίσω σαρκὸς ἑτέρας 'having gone out after different flesh'?

It explains what is meant by the preceding participle ἐκπορνεύσασαι 'having committed sexual immorality' [Blm]: they committed sexual immorality; i.e., they went out after different flesh. It refers to their desire to have sexual relations with the two angels whom Lot had received [BNTC, EBC, TH, WBC]; it refers to homosexuality [Hie, Hu, NTC, TBST, TNTC] and bestiality [Hu]. Others disagree, saying that it cannot mean homosexuality [WBC] and does not include bestiality [Lns].

they-are-set-forth[a] (as-an)-example,[b] experiencing[c] punishment[d] of-eternal fire.

LEXICON—a. pres. mid. (deponent = act.) of πρόκειμαι (LN **13.75**) (BAGD 1. p. 707): 'to be set forth' [Alf; KJV], 'to be set before (one)' [NAB], 'to be set' [AB], 'to be put before (one)' [NJB], 'to exist' [**LN**], 'to exist openly, to exist clearly' [LN], 'to be exhibited' [BAGD, WBC], 'to be displayed' [NET], 'to lie before (the eyes)' [Lns], 'to stand out' [BNTC], 'to serve as' [ISV, NIV, NRSV], 'to be' [NLT], not explicit [REB, TEV, TNT]. This word means to be visible to the eyes [Hie, Lns, NIBC, NTC]; the region was visible [Hie] as evidence of God's judgment [NTC]. The present tense (together with the following αἰωνίου 'eternal' [BNTC]) indicates that the situation was still continuing [BNTC, Lns, TH].

b. δεῖγμα (LN **28.48**) (BAGD 2. p. 172): 'example' [Alf, BAGD, BNTC, LN, WBC; CEV, ISV, KJV, NET, NIV, NJB, NRSV], 'indication' [Lns], 'warning' [NLT, REB, TNT], 'a plain warning' [TEV]. This singular form is translated as plural: 'examples' [AB]. This noun is translated as a phrase: 'to dissuade us' [NAB]. It means a sign pointing to the 'eternal fire' [Lns].

c. pres. act. participle of ὑπέχω (LN **90.68**) (BAGD p. 842): 'to experience' [LN], 'to undergo' [Alf, BAGD, BNTC, LN, Lns, WBC; NAB, NRSV], 'to suffer' [AB, LN; KJV, NET, NIV, TEV, TNT], 'to pay' [NJB, REB], not explicit [CEV, ISV, NLT]. This active participle is translated as a passive: 'to be subjected to' [**LN**]. The present tense implies action continuing to the author's day, suggested by the physical phenomena occurring in the region [Alf, BNTC, EGT, Hie, Hu, Lns, WBC].

d. δίκη (LN 38.8) (BAGD 1. p. 198): 'punishment' [AB, BAGD, BNTC, LN, WBC; ISV, NAB, NET, NIV, NRSV, TEV, TNT], 'just punishment' [Alf], 'penalty' [BAGD; NJB, REB], 'vengeance' [KJV], 'justice' [Lns]. This noun is also translated as a verb: 'to punish' [CEV, NLT].

QUESTION—What is the function of this clause?
1. It states the result of the actions described in the preceding clause [BNTC, TH]: as a result they are set forth . . .
2. It states the function of the cities referred to [NRSV]: these cities serve as an example . . .

QUESTION—Who is the implied causative agent of this clause?
God is the causative agent [CEV].
QUESTION—How are δεῖγμα 'example', πυρὸς αἰωνίου 'eternal fire', and δίκην ὑπέχουσαι 'experiencing punishment' related to each other?
1. Δεῖγμα 'example' is related to δίκην ὑπέχουσαι 'experiencing punishment' [Blm, EGT, Lns; CEV, NAB, NIV, NJB, NRSV]: they are set forth as an example by experiencing punishment.
2. Δεῖγμα 'example' governs πυρὸς αἰωνίου 'eternal fire'; they are set forth as an indication [Lns], a warning [NLT], an example [ISV], a foretaste [TNTC], a figurative representation [Hu] of eternal fire.
3. Πυρὸς αἰωνίου 'eternal fire' is connected with ὑπέχουσαι δίκην 'experiencing punishment' [AB, Alf, BNTC, EGT, El, Hie, ICC, Law, Lg, NTC, WBC; CEV, ISV, KJV, NAB, NET, NIV, NJB, NRSV, REB, TEV, TNT]. The punishment is eternal [El].
   3.1 It states what the punishment is [CEV, NET]: experiencing punishment which is eternal fire.
   3.2 It states where the punishment takes place [REB]: experiencing punishment in eternal fire.
QUESTION—What relationship is indicated by the participle ὑπέχουσαι 'experiencing'?
1. It explains the meaning of δεῖγμα 'example' [Blm, EGT]: they are an example; i.e., they are experiencing.
2. It expresses means [Lns; NET, NRSV]: they are an example by experiencing.
3. It expresses a reason [NJB]: they are an example because they are experiencing.
4. It is temporal [NAB]: they are an example while they are experiencing.
5. It is translated as an attributive [NIV]: they are an example of those who are experiencing.

DISCOURSE UNIT: 8–16 (Hie). The topic is the description of the modern apostates.

DISCOURSE UNIT: 8–13 (BNTC, EBC, Law). The topic is a more circumstantial denunciation [BNTC], description and fate of the false teachers [EBC], the false teachers' record [Law].

DISCOURSE UNIT: 8–11 (NTC). The topic is application and examples.

DISCOURSE UNIT: 8–10 (TNTC; NJB). The topic is the analogies of judgment applied [TNTC], the violent language of the false teachers [NJB].

DISCOURSE UNIT: 8–9 (AB). The topic is triple crimes and their judgment.

8 Similarly,[a] nevertheless,[b] these (persons) also, dreaming,[c] on-the-one-hand defile[d] flesh,[e]
LEXICON—a. ὁμοίως (LN 64.1) (BAGD p.567): 'similarly' [LN; ISV, NAB], 'in similar fashion' [BNTC], 'in similar manner' [Lns], 'in like manner'

[AB, Alf], 'likewise' [LN; KJV], 'in the same way' [BAGD, WBC; NRSV, REB, TEV], 'in the very same way' [NIV], 'are doing the same' [NJB], 'it is just the same with' [TNT], 'just like' [CEV], not explicit [NET, NLT]. This word, being in first position [BNTC, Law], connects the behavior of the persons in this verse with that of the people of Sodom and Gomorrah [BNTC, EBC, Hie, Hu, Law, TH].

b. μέντοι (LN 89.130) (BAGD 2. p. 503): 'nevertheless' [Alf, LN; NJB], 'notwithstanding' [BNTC], 'yet' [Lns, WBC; NET, NLT, NRSV], 'but' [AB, BAGD, LN], 'also' [KJV, TEV], not explicit [CEV, ISV, NAB, NIV, REB, TNT]. It refers to actions done in spite of the warnings [Alf, Blm, BNTC, EGT, El, Hie, Lg, WBC]. It is adversative, implying 'however' [Lg, NIBC, NTC]. It merely emphasizes ὁμοίως 'likewise' [Hu].

c. pres. mid. (deponent = act.) of ἐνυπνιάζομαι (LN 33.487) (BAGD p. 270): 'to dream' [BAGD, LN, Lns], 'to have visions' [TEV], 'to put (oneself) in a trance' [TNT]. This participle is translated as a substantive: 'dreamer' [AB; CEV, ISV, NIV, NRSV], 'deluded dreamer' [REB], 'filthy dreamer' [KJV], 'visionary' [NAB]; as a prepositional phrase: 'in their dreams' [Alf], 'in their dreamings' [BNTC], 'on the strength of their dreams' [WBC], 'as a result of their dreams' [NET], 'in their delusions' [NJB]. The present tense implies ongoing action [Hie, Law, NTC]. It refers to the figurative dreaming in the sleep of sin [Alf, EBC, El], being controlled by delusive fancies [Blm, Hie, Hu, Law, Lg, Lns], having or claiming to have visionary experiences [BNTC, ICC, NIBC, TBST, TG, TH, TNTC, WBC] which justify their sinful acts [TG, TH], their antinomian actions [WBC].

d. pres. act. indic. of μιαίνω (LN 88.260) (BAGD 2. p. 520): 'to defile' [AB, Alf, BAGD, LN, Lns, WBC; ISV, KJV, NET, NJB, NRSV, REB, TNT], 'to stain' [BAGD], 'to contaminate' [LN], 'to pollute' [BNTC; NAB, NIV], 'to cause to be morally filthy' [LN], 'to sin against' [TEV]. It is an immoral use of their sexual powers [TG]. The present tense implies continuing action [Hie, Law].

e. σάρξ (LN 8.4, 8.63): 'flesh' [LN (8.63), Lns], 'body' [LN (8.4)]. Although without the definite article it is nevertheless translated as definite: 'the flesh' [AB, Alf, WBC; KJV, NAB, NET, NRSV]; as a possessive: 'their flesh' [ISV], 'their bodies' [BNTC; NJB, REB, TNT], 'their own bodies' [CEV, NIV, TEV]. It refers to the bodies of the false teachers [EBC]. Without the definite article, it refers to flesh in general [Alf], their own flesh and the flesh of others (strange flesh [Lg]) as well [Hie, Hu, Law, Lg]. This word is emphatic by forefronting. It refers here to the physical body and to the moral nature [Hie].

QUESTION—What is the function of this verse?

It contains the same charges as those in verse 4 [AB]; it refers to the same people as in verse 4 [Hie, Law]; it describes the sins of the false teachers [Hu].

JUDE 1:8 37

QUESTION—What is the reference for καὶ οὗτοι 'these persons also'?
  It refers to the persons mentioned in verse 4 [Hu, ICC, Lg, Lns, TH].
QUESTION—What relationship is indicated by the participle ἐνυπνιαζόμενοι 'dreaming'?
  This participle governs all three of the following phrases [Alf, BNTC, EGT, El, Hie, Hu, Law, Lns, NIBC, NTC, TNTC, WBC].
  1. It is in predicate relationship to οὗτοι 'these persons' [Lns]: these persons also, and they are dreaming, defile . . .
  2. It expresses content [Alf; NJB]: in their dreams.
  3. It expresses the basis or condition of their actions [BNTC, Hu, WBC; NET]: on the basis of their dreams. The false teachers derived their authority from their dreams [NET].
  4. It is translated as a substantive [AB, Blm; CEV, ISV, KJV, NAB, NIV, NRSV, REB]: dreamers/visionaries. However, this would require a definite article since the antecedent, οὗτοι 'these persons' is definite.
  5. It is translated as a finite verb phrase [TEV, TNT]: they have visions.
QUESTION—What is meant by σάρκα μιαίνουσιν 'they defile flesh'?
  This phrase refers to physical and moral defilement [Hie], gross licentiousness [Law], unnatural lusts [Alf], sexual immorality [BNTC, El, NIBC, TH]. It means that they pollute (destroy [CEV]) (sin against [TEV]) their own bodies [BNTC, NTC; CEV, NIV, NJB, REB, TEV, TNT], their flesh [ISV], by sexual excess [NTC, TBST] including homosexuality [BNTC, NTC, TBST]; they live immoral lives [NLT].

on-the-other-hand they-reject[a] lordship,[b] and they-blaspheme[c] glories.[d]
LEXICON—a. pres. act. indic. of ἀθετέω (LN 31.100) (BAGD 1.b. p. 21): 'to reject' [BAGD, LN, WBC; CEV, ISV, NET, NIV, NRSV, TNT], 'to set at nought' [BNTC, Lns], 'to defy' [NLT], 'to spurn' [NAB], 'to despise' [Alf; KJV, TEV], 'to flout' [AB; REB], 'to set aside' [LN], 'to disregard' [NJB], 'not to recognize' [BAGD]. It implies rebellion [Hie]. The present tense implies a continuing attitude [Hie, Law].
  b. κυριότης (LN 12.44, 37.52) (BAGD 2. p. 460): 'lordship' [Alf, Lns], 'ruling power' [LN (37.52)], 'dominion' [KJV], 'God's dominion' [NAB], 'God's authority' [TEV], 'the Lord's authority' [ISV, TNT], 'the authority of the Lord' [WBC], 'authority' [AB, BNTC; CEV, NET, NIV, NLT, NRSV, REB], 'Authority' [NJB], 'glory of the Lord' [BAGD], (various renderings) [LN (12.44)]. Here it includes the authority of Jesus, the angels, and Jude [AB]. It refers to the holy angels [Alf], to the divine majesty [EGT], to the Lordship of God [El, NTC], to the lordship of Christ [NTC, TBST; NET], to the authority of Christ and his Word over his people [Hie, Law]. It is God's authority which may be represented by angels or by human beings [TG]. This word is emphatic by forefronting.
  c. pres. act. indic. of βλασθημέω (LN 33.400) (BAGD 2.c. p. 142): 'to blaspheme' [BAGD, LN, Lns], 'to revile' [BNTC, LN; NAB], 'to slander' [WBC; ISV, NIV, NRSV], 'to scoff at' [NLT], 'to insult' [AB; CEV,

NET, REB, TEV, TNT], 'to speak evil of' [Alf; KJV], 'to abuse' [NJB]. It means here to speak disparagingly [WBC]. The present tense implies continuing practice [Law].

d. δόξα (LN 12.49) (BAGD 4. p. 204): 'glory' [Alf, Lns], 'glorious power' [LN], 'glorious angelic being' [BAGD], 'angel' [CEV, ISV], 'celestial being' [NIV, REB], 'wonderful being' [LN], 'dignity' [KJV]. This plural noun with no definite article is translated as definite: 'the angelic beings' [NAB], 'the Glories' [NJB], 'the glorious ones' [AB, BNTC, WBC; NET, NRSV], 'the glorious ones above' [TNT], 'the glorious beings above' [TEV], 'the power of the glorious ones' [NLT]; as a possessive: '(the Lord's) angels' [ISV]. It refers to angelic beings [BNTC, CBC, EGT, TG, TNTC], good angels [Hie, NIBC, TBST, TH, TNTC, WBC], the holy angels in God's court [AB, Alf, NTC], the attributes and perfections of Christ [Law], Christ's glories [Lns], unseen powers who merit reverence [El], evil angels [Hu; NET]. This word is emphatic by forefronting.

QUESTION—What relationship is indicated by these two clauses?

They refer to an additional side of the sinful nature of the false teachers [Hu]. They state the reason for the preceding statement [TH]: they defile flesh because they reject . . . and blaspheme . . .

QUESTION—What relationship is indicated by the combination of μέν 'on the one hand' in the preceding clause and the two occurrences of δέ 'on the other hand' in this part of the verse?

These three particles balance with each other the three acts referred to [Lns]. The two occurrences of δέ 'on the other hand' balance these two clauses against μέν 'on the one hand' in the preceding clause, contrasting the two latter presumptuous sins against the preceding physical sins [BNTC, Lg(M)], contrasting the first item, dealing with their immoral behavior, with the two following items, dealing with their rejection of authority [WBC], and implying that they occur at the same time [BNTC]. The two uses of δέ 'and' indicate a continuation and a contrast with what precedes, the first changing from the effect on themselves to their attitude toward the authority over them, and the second δέ 'and' changing from reference to Christ to reference to good angels [Hie]. These particles show that the three descriptive clauses are all connected with the participle ἐνυπνιαζόμενοι 'dreaming' [Hie]: dreaming, they defile . . . reject . . . and blaspheme . . .

QUESTION—What is meant by κυριότητα ἀθετοῦσιν 'they reject lordship'?

It means rejection of authority [CEV], of the Lord's authority [ISV], of Jesus as Lord over their lives [EBC, Law, NIBC, TNTC, WBC]. It refers to their doctrine of God and of Christ [BNTC].

QUESTION—What is meant by δόξας βλασφημοῦσιν 'they blaspheme glories'?

It refers to the tradition that the law of God was given at Sinai by angels, and rejection of angels here implies rejection of obedience to God's law [TBST, TNTC, WBC].

DISCOURSE UNIT: 9–10 (TBST). The topic is warnings of judgment: a familiar example.

9 **But Michael the archangel, when, contending[a] with-the Devil, he-was-disputing[b] concerning[c] the body of-Moses,**

LEXICON—a. pres. mid. (deponent = act.) participle of διακρίνομαι (LN 33.444) (BAGD 2.a. p. 185): 'to contend' [Alf, Lns; KJV, NRSV], 'to dispute' [BAGD, BNTC, LN], 'to argue' [AB; NET], 'to fight' [ISV], 'to take issue' [BAGD], 'to debate about' [LN]. This participle is also translated as a prepositional phrase: 'in debate' [WBC], 'in his dispute' [**LN**], 'in his quarrel' [TEV], 'when his case was being judged' [NAB]. The phrase ὅτε διακρινόμενος . . . διελέγετο 'when contending . . . he was disputing' is conflated: 'when (the two of them) were arguing' [CEV], 'when he was engaged in argument' [NJB], 'when he was disputing' [NIV, REB], 'when he was arguing' [NLT], 'in his argument' [TNT]. The combination of these two words strengthens the concept [Hu]. This word implies contending [Lns], disputing [EGT], getting a dispute decided [ICC], a dispute in law [ICC, Lg, NIBC, WBC]. It refers to Michael's challenge to the Devil's claim on the body of Moses [TH]. The present tense implies a continuing encounter [Hie, Law, NTC] occurring at the same time as the verb διελέγετο 'he was disputing' [NTC]. The prefixed preposition δια- implies 'between' and emphasizes the back-and-forth confrontation [Hie, Lns].

b. imperf. mid. (deponent = act.) indic. of διαλέγομαι (LN 33.446) (BAGD 1. p. 185): 'to dispute' [AB, Alf, LN, WBC; KJV, NRSV], 'to argue' [LN; TEV], 'to debate' [NET], 'to be at odds' [BNTC], 'to exchange words' [Lns], 'to discuss' [BAGD]. This word is also translated as a noun: 'a dispute' [AB; NAB]. (See a. for those conflating this with the preceding participle [CEV, NIV, NJB, NLT, REB, TNT].) This word shows that the conflict was in words [Hie, Hu, Law, Lg]. The prefixed preposition δια- implies 'between' and emphasizes the confrontational position of the two [Hie]. The imperfect tense indicates continuation in past time [NTC].

c. περί with genitive object (LN 90.24): 'concerning' [Alf, LN; NET], 'about' [BNTC, LN, Lns, WBC; CEV, KJV, NIV, NJB, NLT, NRSV, TNT], 'over' [AB; ISV, NAB], 'for the possession of' [REB], 'about who would have' [TEV].

QUESTION—What is the function of this verse?

It emphasizes the wickedness of the false teachers' blasphemies by speaking against the 'glories' as Michael did not dare to speak against the Devil [Hu, Lg].

QUESTION—What relationship is indicated by δέ 'but'?

It introduces a strong contrast with the preceding statement [Hie; NET].

QUESTION—What relationship is indicated by the participle διακρινόμενος 'disputing'?
1. It is translated as a parallel action to διελέγετο 'he was discussing' [AB; ISV, NET, NRSV]: when he was disputing and discussing.
2. The participle διακρινόμενος 'disputing' and the verb διελέγετο 'he was discussing' are combined into one concept [CEV, NIV, NJB, NLT, REB, TEV, TNT]: when he was disputing.
3. It is translated as being governed by ὅτε 'when' and therefore temporal [Hie]: when contending with the Devil. (However, ὅτε 'when' governs the finite verb διελέγετο 'he was disputing', not this participle.)

QUESTION—What is implied by the term τῷ διαβόλῳ 'the Devil'?
The Greek word means 'the slanderer' and makes prominent the evil character of Satan [Hie].

he-dared[a] not bring-against[b] (him) a-judgment[c] of-blasphemy,[d]

LEXICON—a. aorist act. indic. of τολμάω (LN **25.161**) (BAGD 1.b. . 822): 'to dare' [AB, Alf, LN; all versions except NAB, REB], 'to venture' [Lns; NAB], 'to presume' [BNTC, WBC; REB], 'to bring oneself' [BAGD]. The aorist tense refers to a definite occasion [Law].
b. aorist act. infin. of ἐπιφέρω (LN 90.94) (BAGD 3. p. 304): 'to bring against' [Alf, Lns; KJV, NIV, NRSV], 'to bring upon' [LN], 'to bring' [AB; ISV, NET], 'to impose upon' [LN], 'to pronounce' [BAGD, BNTC], not explicit [WBC; CEV, NAB, NJB, NLT, REB, TEV, TNT]. The aorist tense refers to a definite occasion [Law].
c. κρίσις (LN 30.110) (BAGD 1.b.β. p. 453): 'judgment' [AB, Alf, BAGD, BNTC, LN; NET], 'judging' [Lns], 'accusation' [ISV, KJV, NIV], 'condemnation' [NRSV], 'decision, evaluation' [LN], not explicit [CEV]. This noun is also translated as a verb: 'to charge' [NAB], 'to accuse' [NLT], 'to condemn' [WBC; REB, TEV, TNT], 'to denounce' [NJB]. It refers to a verdict [Hie, Hu, Law]; it implies condemnation [Lg]. It implies an action [Lns].
d. βλασφημία (LN 33.400, 33.401) (BAGD 2.a.β. p. 143): 'blasphemy' [LN (33.401), Lns; NAB, NLT], 'slander' [WBC; NRSV], 'insult' [AB; TNT], 'evil speaking' [Alf], 'language of abuse' [NJB], 'insulting words' [REB, TEV]. This noun is also translated as an adjective: 'slanderous' [ISV, NET, NIV]; as a participle: 'reviling' [BAGD, BNTC, LN (33.400)], 'railing' [KJV]; as a verb: 'to insult' [CEV].

QUESTION—What is implied by this clause?
1. Michael did not dare to utter a blasphemy against the Devil [Alf, BAGD, Blm, BNTC, CBC, EBC, EGT, El, Hie, Hu, Law, Lg, LN, Lns, NIBC, NTC, TH; ISV, KJV, NIV, NJB, TEV, TNT], by condemning the Devil [Law, Lns]. Michael refrained because Satan was a celestial being, although fallen [CBC, EBC, EGT], because of Michael's reverence for Satan's former glory [Alf, El]. Michael refrained in recognition of the Devil's deadly and dangerous character [Law]. Michael, himself a created

being, refused to assume the prerogative of God by condemning the Devil [Hie, Law, Lns, TH]. Michael refrained in great dread of God's majesty [Lg].
2. Michael did not dare to make a legal decision about Satan's accusation against Moses [TBST].

QUESTION—What is the implied predicate of ἐπενεγκεῖν 'bring against'?
1. The implied predicate is 'him', i.e., the Devil [Alf; CEV, ISV, KJV, NAB, NIV, NJB, NLT, NRSV, REB, TEV, TNT]: to bring against the Devil.
2. The implied predicate is the insult made by the Devil [AB]: to bring against the insult.

QUESTION—How are the two nouns related in the genitive construction κρίσιν βλασφημίας 'a judging of blasphemy'?
1. The genitive noun βλασφημίας 'of blasphemy' refers to what Michael refrained from speaking [Alf, BAGD, Blm, BNTC, CBC, EBC, EGT, El, Hie, Hu, Law, Lg, LN, Lns, NIBC; ISV, KJV, NET, NIV, NJB, TEV, TNT].
   1.1 It describes κρίσιν 'judgment' [Alf, BAGD, Blm, BNTC, CBC, EBC, EGT, El, Hie, LN, Lns, NIBC; ISV, KJV, NET, NIV, TEV]: a reviling judgment.
   1.2 It states how the judgment would have been expressed [Hu, Law, Lg; NJB, TEV, TNT]: to condemn him with blasphemous words.
2. The genitive noun βλασφημίας 'of blasphemy' refers to the Devil's blasphemy [AB, CBC, ICC, TBST, WBC; NAB, NLT], claiming that Moses was a murderer [CBC, ICC].
   2.1 Michael did not dare to bring judgment against Satan's words [AB, ICC, WBC; NAB, NLT]: to charge him with blasphemy. Michael would not reject the Devil's accusations on his own authority [WBC].
   2.2 Michael did not dare to join the Devil's accusation against Moses [TBST].

but said, "(The) Lord rebuke[a] you."

LEXICON—a. aorist act. optative of ἐπιτιμάω (LN 33.419) (BAGD 1. p. 303): 'to rebuke' [Alf, BAGD, BNTC, LN, Lns, WBC; all versions except CEV, ISV, NAB], 'to reprimand' [ISV], 'to denounce' [LN], 'to punish' [NAB]. This optative verb is translated as a future indicative, 'will rebuke' [AB], 'will punish' [CEV].

QUESTION—What relationship is indicated by ἀλλά 'but'?
It introduces the contrast between what Michael did not do and what he did do [Hie]: he did not bring against him . . . but he did say . . . Michael's mild response to an evil celestial being emphasizes the appalling arrogance of the false teachers' blasphemies against good angels [Hie, Hu].

DISCOURSE UNIT: 10–13 [AB]. The topic is a triple example of deviants judged.

JUDE 1:10

10 **But these (persons), on-the-one-hand as-many-things-as they-know[a] not they-blaspheme,[b]**

LEXICON—a. perf. (with present meaning) act. indic. of οἶδα (LN 28.1, 32.4): 'to know' [AB, Alf, LN (28.1), Lns; KJV], 'to know about' [CEV], 'to have knowledge of' [NAB], 'to understand' [BNTC, LN (32.4), WBC; ISV, NET, NIV, NJB, NLT, NRSV, REB, TEV, TNT], 'to comprehend' [LN (32.4)]. This verb refers to innate knowledge [NTC]. With the negative οὐκ 'not' here, it implies that the knowledge is not intelligible to them [Hie]; they know about it but have no comprehensive knowledge of it [Hu].

   b. pres. act. indic. of βλασφημέω (LN 33.400) (BAGD 2.c. p. 142): 'to blaspheme' [BAGD, LN, Lns], 'to slander' [WBC; ISV, NET, NRSV], 'to defame' [LN], 'to speak evil of' [Alf; KJV], 'to revile' [BNTC, LN; NAB], 'to mock and curse' [NLT], 'to speak abusively against' [NIV], 'to pour abuse on' [REB], 'to abuse' [NJB], 'to insult' [AB; CEV, TNT], 'to attack with insults' [TEV]. The present tense indicates habitual actions [Hie]. Here it refers to insulting [TH].

QUESTION—What relationship is indicated by δέ 'but'?

It states a strong contrast with the preceding comment concerning Michael [El, Hu]. The use of μέν 'on the one hand' in this clause and δέ 'on the other hand' in the following clause constitute two balanced statements [Hie], an antithesis [Lg(M)].

QUESTION—What relationship is indicated by οὗτοι 'these persons'?

It is used disparagingly [AB, BNTC, EBC, Hie] here and in verses 8, (11 [AB]), 12, 16, and 19 [AB, BNTC]. It refers back to the persons mentioned in verse 8 [TH]. With δέ 'on the other hand', it indicates a change of subject [NTC].

QUESTION—To whom does ὅσα οὐκ οἴδασιν 'as many things as they know not' refer?

It refers to powers [CEV], the spiritual world [Alf, EGT, El, Hie, Hu, ICC, Lg, TH], spiritual matters [NIBC], angels [BAGD, Hie, NIBC, TH] including the δόξαι 'glories' [ICC, Lg, Lns] and κυριότης 'lordship' mentioned in verse 8 [ICC], God's authority [TH], the glories of Christ and whatever is beyond their knowledge [Law, Lns], the revealed truths of the Christian faith [NET]. It refers to the same thing as δόξας 'glories' in verse 8 [EGT, El, Hu].

on-the-other-hand as-many-things-as they-understand[a] naturally[b] as/like[c] the unreasoning[d] animals,[e]

LEXICON—a. pres. mid. (deponent = act.) indic. of ἐπίσταμαι (LN 28.3, 32.3) (BAGD 2. p. 300): 'to understand' [AB, Alf, LN (32.3), Lns, WBC; NIV, NJB, REB, TNT], 'to be aware of' [LN (32.2)], 'to know' [BAGD, BNTC, LN (28.3); ISV, KJV, NAB, NRSV, TEV], 'to know really' [LN (32.3)], 'to comprehend' [NET], 'to be acquainted with' [BAGD]. The phrase ὅσα δὲ φυσικῶς ἐπίστανται 'on the other hand as many things as

they understand naturally' is translated 'they do whatever their instincts tell them' [NLT]. This entire clause and the following clause is translated 'they are like senseless animals that end up getting destroyed, because they live only by their feelings' [CEV]. This phrase refers to the same thing as σάρκα 'flesh' in verse 8 [EGT]. This word refers to knowledge resulting from practical experience [El, Law]. This word and the preceding οἴδασιν 'they know' are essentially synonymous and are distinguished only by the present context, the present verb implying here mere external knowledge [Hu]; this word is stronger than the preceding οἴδασιν 'they know' and is ironical [Lg]. The things they know are fleshly delights [ICC]. These things are sexual instincts like the instinctive behavior of animals in heat [NET].
- b. φυσικῶς (LN **58.9**) (BAGD p. 869): 'naturally' [Alf, BAGD, LN; KJV], 'by nature' [AB, LN; NJB], 'in a purely natural manner' [BNTC], 'by instinct' [BAGD, **LN**; ISV, NAB, NIV, NRSV, TEV, TNT], 'instinctively' [WBC; NET], 'by their senses' [REB], 'physically' [Lns].
- c. ὡς (LN 64.12): 'as' [Alf, LN, Lns; KJV, TNT], 'like' [AB, BNTC, LN, WBC; ISV, NAB, NET, NIV, NLT, NRSV, REB, TEV].
- d. ἄλογος (LN 30.12) (BAGD 1. p. 41): 'unreasoning' [BAGD, WBC; NIV, NJB], 'unable to reason, not able to reason' [LN], 'without reason' [AB, LN], 'irrational' [Alf, Lns; ISV, NET, NRSV], 'senseless' [CEV], 'brute' [BNTC; KJV, NAB, REB], 'wild' [TEV, TNT], not specific [NLT]. In this context it means 'wild' [TH].
- e. ζῷον (LN 4.2) (BAGD 2. p. 341): 'animal' [AB, Alf, BAGD, LN, Lns, WBC; all versions except KJV, REB], 'beast' [BNTC; KJV, REB], 'living creature' [LN]. The phrase ἄλογα ζῷα 'unreasoning animals' is the regular term for the animal world [NIBC, WBC]; it is not disparaging [NIBC].

QUESTION—What relationship is indicated by δέ 'on the other hand'?

It introduces a strong contrast between the objects referred to [Hie], a contrast to the preceding clause [El, Hu], stating the other side of the situation [Hie].

QUESTION—What relationship is indicated by ὡς 'as/like'?
1. It indicates manner [AB, Alf, BNTC, EBC, Hie, ICC, Lg, Lns, WBC; all versions except CEV, KJV, NET]: as unreasoning animals do.
2. It indicates similarity [CEV, NET]: they are like unreasoning animals.

in[a] these (things) they-are-destroyed/they-destroy-themselves.[b]

LEXICON—a. ἐν with dative object (LN 83.13, 89.76): 'in' [AB, Alf, LN (83.13); KJV], 'in connection with' [Lns], 'by' [BNTC, LN (89.76), WBC; ISV, NET, NRSV], 'by means of' [LN (89.76)], 'through' [NAB], 'because' [CEV], not explicit [NIV, NJB, NLT, REB, TEV, TNT]. This preposition is instrumental, meaning 'by' [Hie].
- b. pres. pass./mid. indic. of φθείρω (LN 20.23, 20.39) (BAGD 2.c. p. 857): 'to be destroyed' [AB, BAGD, LN (20.39), WBC; CEV, ISV, NET,

NRSV], 'to be brought to destruction' [BNTC], 'to be corrupted' [NAB], 'to be ruined' [LN (20.23)]; as a middle voice: 'to corrupt oneself' [Alf; KJV], 'to bring about one own destruction' [NLT], 'to bring about one's ruin' [TNT], 'to perish' [Lns]. This verb is also translated actively with 'these things' as the subject: 'to destroy' [NIV, TEV], 'to prove one's undoing' [REB], 'to turn out to be fatal' [NJB]. It refers to self-ruin [El, Hu], and the present tense indicates that it is going on now [El, Hie], culminating in eternal ruin [Hie]. It refers to judgment [WBC], to condemnation by God [BNTC, EBC, NIBC, TH] on the day of judgment [BNTC]. This entire clause is translated 'these are the very things that destroy them' [NIV], 'and they bring about their own destruction' [NLT], 'bring about their ruin' [TNT], 'will turn out to be fatal to them' [NJB], 'are the very things that destroy them' [TEV], 'prove their undoing' [REB].

QUESTION—What is implied by this clause?

The destruction comes because they are doing these things [TH].

DISCOURSE UNIT: 11–16 [NJB]. The topic is the false teachers' vicious behavior.

DISCOURSE UNIT: 11–13 [TBST, TNTC, WBC]. The topic is warnings of judgment [TBST]: three more OT examples [TBST, TNTC, WBC].

11 Woe^a to them, because in-the way of Cain they-have-gone

LEXICON—a. οὐαί (LN 22.9): 'woe' [AB, Alf, BNTC, Lns, WBC; KJV, NET, NIV, NRSV], 'alas' [NJB, REB], 'disaster, horror' [LN]. The phrase οὐαὶ αὐτοῖς 'woe to them' is translated 'What a tragedy!' [TNT], 'So much the worse for them!' [NAB], 'How terrible for them!' [TEV], 'How terrible it will be for them!' [ISV, NLT], 'Now they are in for real trouble' [CEV]. It implies a threat [Hu, Lg] and disapproval [Hu; TNT]. It is a declaration of doom [Law, Lns, TH; CEV, ISV, NAB, NJB, NLT, TEV].

QUESTION—What relationship is indicated by ὅτι 'because'?

It indicates the reason that there will be woe to them [Hie, TH].

QUESTION—How are the two nouns related in the genitive construction τῇ ὁδῷ τοῦ Κάϊν 'in the way of Cain'?

The genitive noun Κάϊν 'Cain' states who went in the way [NAB, TEV]: the way in which Cain went. They do the same as Cain did [TG].

QUESTION—To what does τῇ ὁδῷ τοῦ Κάϊν 'in the way of Cain' refer?

It refers to selfishness [Alf, EGT, Hie, NTC] and envy [Alf, Hie], greed and hatred of God and mankind [NTC], acting in self-interest against God's warnings [Hu, Lg], defying God and despising people [TNTC], godlessness and moral irresponsibility [BNTC], religious error [EBC], religious unbelief [Law], immorality and denial of future judgment [WBC], wickedness in general [CBC, Lns], treachery and greed [TG]. It refers to deciding for themselves whether to accept God's standards [TBST], antinomianism

JUDE 1:11   45

[NIBC]. The dative τῇ ὁδῷ 'in the way' is a dative of direction [Lg], of place [NTC].

QUESTION—What relationship is indicated by ἐπορεύθησαν 'they have gone'?
  1. It is prophetic, anticipating their destiny as certain [Law, Lg].
  2. It refers to a recently begun occurrence [Lns].

and in-the error[a] of Balaam for-wages[b] they-have-plunged-into[c]

LEXICON—a. πλάνη (LN 31.8, 31.10) (BAGD p. 666): 'error' [Alf, BAGD, BNTC, LN (31.10), Lns, WBC; all versions except CEV, NJB, NLT], 'misleading belief' [LN (31.10)], 'deceptive belief' [LN (31.10)], 'delusion' [NJB], 'deception' [LN (31.8)], 'mistake' [CEV], 'deceit' [AB], not explicit [NLT]. This word has an active meaning, implying that the false teachers were the actors [NTC]. The false teachers' error, like Balaam's, was deceiving the people [NTC], encouraging the people in sinful desires [Blm, CBC, Lg], sinning and leading others to sin, for the sake of money [TH, TNTC, WBC], leading people into false teachings and immorality [EBC, EGT, Hie], seeking self-exaltation [EGT], and devoted to the love of money [EBC, Hie, Hu, Lg, NIBC, NTC], going against God's will for selfish advantage [El, Hu, TBST], covetous unbelief [Law], antinomianism [NIBC, TBST]; they are driven by the same weakness as Balaam, being willing to do anything for financial gain and making money by their teaching [BNTC]. This word is forefronted for emphasis [Law]. The dative case indicates direction [Lg], means or manner [EGT].

b. μισθός (LN 38.14, 57.173, 90.89) (BAGD 1. p. 523): 'wages' [LN (57.173), Lns], 'pay' [BAGD, LN (57.173); NAB], 'gain' [AB, BAGD; NRSV], 'money' [CEV, NLT, TEV, TNT], 'recompense' [LN (38.14)], 'reward' [Alf, LN; KJV, NJB], 'profit' [BNTC, WBC; NIV, REB], 'to make a profit' [ISV]. The phrase 'for wages' is translated 'because of greed' [NET]. This genitive noun is a genitive of price [Alf, BAGD, El, Hu, Lns, NTC], of quality [NIBC].

c. aorist pass. (deponent = act.)/pass. indic. of ἐκχέω (ἐκχέομαι LN **41.13**, 47.4, **68.75, 90.82**) (BAGD 3. p. 247): 'to plunge into' [LN (68.75, **90.82**); REB], 'to rush into' [NIV], 'to rush after' [Alf], 'to rush headlong into' [ISV], 'to go headlong into' [TNT], 'to run greedily after' [KJV], 'to become fully involved in' [LN (**90.82**)]; translated as a passive voice: 'to be poured out' [LN (47.4)]; translated as a middle voice: 'to give oneself over to' [TEV], 'to give (oneself) completely to' [LN (41.13)], 'to give (oneself) over completely to' [LN (**68.75**)], 'to commit (oneself) totally to' [LN (68.75)], 'to give (oneself)' [BAGD], 'to abandon (oneself)' [AB, BAGD, BNTC; NAB, NET, NRSV], 'to throw (oneself) into' [NJB], 'to pour (oneself) out' [Lns]. It implies plunging into [BNTC, Hu, ICC, Law, Lg(M)] or wallowing in [BNTC], running greedily after [El], abandoning oneself to [NTC]. The aorist tense of all three verbs in this verse imply the certainty of the coming destruction of these false teachers [El, Hie]; they imply that the action has recently begun [Lns]; they have the sense of the perfect tense, referring to actions begun in the past with present and continuing effects [TH].

QUESTION—How are the two nouns related in the genitive construction τῇ πλάνῃ τοῦ Βαλαάμ 'in the error of Balaam'?

The genitive noun Βαλαάμ 'Balaam' states who made the error [Blm; CEV, TEV]: the error that Balaam committed.

and in-the rebellion[a] of Korah they-have-perished.[b]

LEXICON—a. ἀντιλογία (LN **39.35**) (BAGD 2. p. 75): 'rebellion' [AB, BAGD, BNTC, LN; ISV, NAB, NET, NIV, NJB, NLT, NRSV], 'defiance' [**LN**], 'contradiction' [Lns], 'gainsaying' [Alf; KJV], 'controversy' [WBC]. This entire phrase is translated 'they have rebelled like Korah, and they share his fate' [REB], 'like Korah they have rebelled and perished' [TNT], 'they have rebelled as Korah rebelled, and like him they are destroyed' [TEV], 'they have also rebelled against God, just as Korah did. Because of all this, they will be destroyed' [CEV]. The dative implies being included in [Alf, Law]. The rebellion was blasphemous insubordination against legitimate authority [BNTC, CBC, Hie, Hu, Law], defiance of church authorities [ICC, NIBC, TH, TNTC], contempt for sacred decrees [El], rebellion against God and his decrees [Lg, Lns, TBST], rebellious unbelief [Law], denial of the divine authority of the Law [WBC], rejection of apostolic leadership and teaching [NTC], coveting positions they have no right to occupy [TH]. The dative case expresses means [Lns, NTC].

b. aorist mid. indic. of ἀπόλλυμι (LN 20.31): 'to perish' [Alf, BNTC, Lns, WBC; KJV, NAB, NET, NJB, NLT, NRSV, TNT], 'to destroy (oneself)' [ISV]; translated as a passive voice: 'to be ruined' [LN; NJB], 'to be destroyed' [AB, LN; CEV, NIV, TEV]. The aorist tense implies that the perishing is already settled [BNTC, EBC], is certain and final [Law, NIBC, NTC, WBC]; it refers to the culmination of the ruin [Hie]; it implies that the action has recently begun [Lns]; it makes the false teachers participants in Korah's rebellion [TBST]. It means that they rebelled like Korah rebelled and they will be destroyed as Korah was destroyed [TG].

QUESTION—How are the two nouns related in the genitive construction τῇ ἀντιλογίᾳ τοῦ Κόρε 'in the rebellion of Korah'?

The genitive noun Κόρε 'Korah' states who rebelled [CEV, NJB, REB, TEV, TNT]: Korah rebelled.

DISCOURSE UNIT: 12–25 [CBC]. The topic is a warning to beware of false teachers.

DISCOURSE UNIT: 12–16 [NTC]. The topic is descriptions.

DISCOURSE UNIT: 12–13 [Hie]. The topic is the figurative description of the false teachers' character.

12 These-persons are the-(ones) feasting-with-(you)/feasting-together[a] (who are) blemishes/rocks[b] in[c] your love-feasts[d] fearlessly[e] shepherding[f] themselves,

TEXT—Some manuscripts omit οἱ 'the (ones)'. GNT does not deal with this variant. This word is clearly omitted by Blm and doubtless by KJV; it appears to be omitted in translation by AB, NAB, NET, NIV, NJB, NLT, NRSV, REB, TEV, TNT (CEV, ISV, KJV are unclear), but it is not clear whether these follow the textual omission or whether the omission is merely stylistic.

LEXICON—a. pres. mid. (deponent = act.) of συνευωχέομαι (LN **23.14**) (BAGD p. 789): 'to feast with (someone)' [AB, Alf, WBC; ISV, KJV, NET, NRSV], 'to feast together' [BAGD, LN], 'to feast along with (someone)' [Lns], 'to eat with (someone)' [NIV], 'to carouse with (someone)' [BNTC], 'to join in (one's) solemn feast' [NAB], 'to join (someone) in a fellowship meal' [NLT], 'to share (one's) table' [TNT], 'to come for the food' [NJB]. In this context this word has a derogatory sense [TH]. The present tense indicates repeated actions [Hie].
  b. σπιλάς (LN **21.5, 79.57**): 'blemish' [NIV, NRSV], 'blotch' [NAB], 'spot' [KJV], 'dirty spot' [LN (79.57); TEV], 'filth spots' [Lns], 'stain' [AB; ISV], 'menace' [TNT], 'rock' [Alf], 'hidden rock' [BNTC], 'hidden danger' [LN (**21.5**)], 'unseen danger' [LN (21.5)], 'dangerous reef' [WBC; NET], 'dangerous reef that can shipwreck (someone)' [NLT], 'dangerous hazard' [NJB], 'danger' [REB]. This entire clause is translated 'These people are filthy minded, and by their shameful and selfish actions they spoil the meals you eat together' [CEV]. This word means 'stain' [Blm, Hu, ICC, Lg]; it means 'rock' [EGT, El, Law, Lg(M), NIBC, TNTC], 'hidden rock' [Hie].
  c. ἐν with dative object (LN 83.13): 'in' [Alf, LN, Lns; KJV, NLT, TEV], 'on' [AB; ISV, NAB, NRSV], 'at' [BNTC, WBC; NET, NIV, NJB, REB], 'to' [TNT].
  d. ἀγάπη (LN **23.28**) (BAGD II. p. 6): 'love-feast' [Alf, BAGD, BNTC; ISV, NET, NIV, NRSV, REB, TNT], '*agape*' [Lns], 'feast of charity' [KJV], 'fellowship meal' [AB, LN, WBC; TEV], 'meal (people) eat together' [CEV], 'community meal' [NJB], 'Christian banquet' [NAB], 'fellowship meal celebrating the love of the Lord' [NLT].
  e. ἀφόβως (LN **53.60, 88.151**) (BAGD 1. p. 127): 'fearlessly' [AB, Alf], 'without fear' [Lns; KJV, NRSV], 'without shame' [NAB, TNT], 'shamelessly' [BAGD, LN (**53.60**)], 'quite shamelessly' [NJB], 'shamefully, disgracefully' [LN (88.151)], 'without the slightest qualm' [NIV], 'without reverence' [BAGD, LN (53.60), WBC; NET], 'without any sense of awe' [ISV], 'without reverence for God' [LN (**53.60**)], 'boldly' [BAGD], 'brazenly' [BNTC]. The phrase συνευωχούμενοι

ἀφόβως 'feasting with you fearlessly' is translated 'with their shameless feasting' [LN (**88.151**)], 'with their shameless carousals' [REB], 'they are shameless in the way they care only about themselves' [NLT]; this phrase is not explicit [TEV]. It implies arrogance [TNTC].
- f. pres. act. participle of ποιμαίνω (LN 44.3) (BAGD 2.b. p. 684): 'to shepherd' [LN], 'to shepherd (oneself)' [Lns], 'to pasture (oneself)' [AB, Alf], 'to look after (oneself)' [BAGD, BNTC, WBC; NAB, NJB], 'to feed (oneself)' [KJV, NET, NRSV], 'to care about (oneself)' [NLT]. The phrase ἑαυτοὺς ποιμαίνοντες 'shepherding themselves' is translated 'shepherds who feed only themselves' [NIV], 'They care only for themselves' [TNT], 'they take care only of themselves' [TEV], 'They are shepherds who care only for themselves' [ISV], 'They are shepherds who take care only of themselves' [REB]. It means here to fatten, to indulge [EGT]. The present tense implies regular practice [Law].

QUESTION—What relationship is indicated by οὗτοι 'these persons'?

It implies disparagement, as in verses 8 and 10 [BNTC, NIBC] and in verses 14, 16, and 19 [NIBC]. It indicates a continuation of the denunciation [Hie].

QUESTION—What relationship is indicated by the participial phrase οἱ ... συνευωχούμενοι 'the ones feasting with you'?

1. It is attributive [BNTC, Lns, WBC]: the ones who feast with you.
2. The following do not relate the masculine article οἱ 'the (ones)' to the masculine participle συνευωχούμενοι 'feasting with you'.
2.1 The article is ignored or omitted [AB, Blm; all versions].
2.1.1 The participle is translated as temporal [Blm, Hie; KJV, NLT, NRSV]: while/when they feast together.
2.1.2 The participle states the reason [LN]: because they are feasting with you.
2.1.3 The participle states the means [REB]: by means of their feasting with you.
2.1.4 The participle is translated as an independent proposition [AB; ISV, NAB, TNT]: they feast with you.
3. The masculine definite article οἱ 'the (ones)' is taken to modify the prepositional phrase ἐν ταῖς ἀγάπαις ὑμῶν 'in your love-feasts' [Alf]: blemishes/rocks which are in your love-feasts.
4. The masculine definite article οἱ 'the (ones)' is taken to modify the feminine noun σπιλάδες 'blemishes/rocks' [Alf, El, Hie, ICC]: these are the blemishes/rocks. . . . This is defended on the grounds that the feminine noun σπιλάδες 'blemishes/rocks' actually refers to the (masculine) false teachers [Hie, ICC].

QUESTION—What is the implied predicate of συνευωχούμενοι 'feasting with you/together'?

1. 'With you' is implied [AB, Alf, BNTC, El, Hie, Hu, Law, Lg, Lns, NIBC, WBC; ISV, KJV, NAB, NIV, NLT, NRSV, TNT] by the prefix συν- [Hie]: feasting with you.

1.1 This implies that the false teachers were members of the church [BNTC].
1.2 They were participating in the love-feasts without being entitled to do so [Law, Lg(M)].
2. It has no predicate and implies 'feasting together' by themselves [ICC].

QUESTION—What is σπιλάδες 'blemishes/rocks' connected with?
1. It is attributive to οἱ συνευωχούμενοι 'the ones feasting with you' [BNTC, Lns] as its position in the phrase shows: the ones feasting with you who are blemishes/rocks in your love-feasts.
2. It is in apposition with οἱ συνευωχούμενοι 'the ones feasting with you' [EGT, WBC]: the ones feasting with you, like blemishes/rocks.

QUESTION—What relationship is indicated by the participial phrase ἑαυτοὺς ποιμαίνοντες 'shepherding themselves'?

It implies selfishness [TNTC]; they care for no one but themselves [AB, Alf, EBC, NIBC, TH, WBC; all versions except CEV, KJV, NRSV]; they feed only themselves [El, Lns, NIBC] instead of feeding the poorer members [El]; they ignore the spiritual purpose of the love-feasts and use them as occasions for their selfish purposes [BNTC, Hie, Law, TBST, WBC]. Although they claim to be church leaders, they do not care for the church members and expect financial support from them [WBC]. The reference is to their general conduct, not merely at the love-feasts [Lg, TH].
1. It is an attendant circumstance to οἱ συνευωχούμενοι 'the ones feasting with you' [Alf; KJV, NJB, NRSV]: they are feasting . . . and also shepherding themselves.
2. It is translated as an attributive participle [NIV]: who shepherd themselves.
3. It is translated as an independent proposition [AB, Hie, WBC; ISV, NAB, NLT, REB, TEV, TNT]: they shepherd themselves.

QUESTION—What is ἀφόβως 'fearlessly' connected with?
1. It is connected with συνευωχούμενοι 'feasting with you' [AB, Alf, El, Law, Lg, TH, WBC; ISV, NET, NIV, NRSV, REB, TNT] feasting with you fearlessly. They participated in the Lord's supper without regarding its sanctity [NET].
2. It is connected with ἑαυτοὺς ποιμαίνοντες 'shepherding themselves' [BNTC, EGT, Hie, ICC; KJV, NJB, NLT]: fearlessly shepherding themselves.
2.1 The reference is to their conduct at the love-feasts [BNTC].
2.2 They defy their rulers' authority and set themselves up as their own shepherds [ICC].

waterless[a] clouds being-carried-along[b] by[c] winds,

TEXT—Instead of παραφερόμεναι 'being carried along', some manuscripts read περιφερόμεναι 'being carried around'. GNT does not deal with this variant. These two words are similar in meaning, but περιφερόμεναι 'being carried around' is doubtless read by KJV and probably by no others.

50   JUDE 1:12

LEXICON—a. ἄνυδρος (LN **2.8**) (BAGD p. 76): 'waterless' [BNTC, LN, Lns; ISV, NET, NRSV], 'without water' [Alf; KJV], 'without rain' [NIV], 'without giving rain' [WBC; NLT, REB], 'that give no rain' [**LN**], 'that yield no rain' [BAGD], 'that bring no rain' [NAB], 'bringing no rain' [NJB, TEV, TNT], 'never bringing any rain' [CEV], 'rainless' [AB], 'dry' [LN]. They drop no water [ICC].
    b. pres. pass. participle of παραφέρω (LN **15.162**) (BAGD 2.a. p. 623): 'to be carried along' [**LN**; NET, NRSV, REB, TEV, TNT], 'to be carried aside' [Lns], 'to be carried out of course' [Alf], 'to be driven along' [LN], 'to be blown along' [WBC; CEV, NIV], 'to be blown about' [ISV, NJB], 'to be blown' [NAB], 'to be carried away' [BAGD], 'to be borne' [AB]; probably different text: 'to be carried about' [KJV]. The phrase ὑπὸ ἀνέμων παραφερόμεναι 'being carried along by winds' is translated 'scurrying before the winds' [BNTC], 'blowing over dry land' [NLT]. The prefix παρα- implies being driven past [Hu, ICC], being carried off the right course and that it is unsafe to follow these teachers [Hie].
    c. ὑπό with genitive object (LN 90.1) (BAGD 1.a.β. p. 843): 'by' [AB, Alf, BAGD, LN, Lns, WBC; all versions except KJV, NAB, NLT], 'of' [KJV], 'on' [NAB].

QUESTION—What is implied by this phrase?
    It implies that the false teachers have nothing to offer to their hearers [BNTC, EBC, El, Hie, Lg, Lns, NIBC, TH, WBC].

QUESTION—To what does the phrase νεφέλαι ἄνυδροι 'waterless clouds' refer?
    It refers to the false teachers' conduct in general, their inability to bring about anything good [Hu, Law, NIBC, NTC, TBST, TH, TNTC], and their deceitfulness [Hu, NIBC]. The point of comparison is worthlessness [TG].

QUESTION—What relationship is indicated by the participle παραφερόμεναι 'being carried along'?
    1. It is probably attributive to νεφέλαι ἄνυδροι 'waterless clouds' [AB; CEV, ISV, NJB, NLT, NRSV, REB, TEV, TNT]: waterless clouds which are being carried along.
    2. It may be a predicate complement to νεφέλαι ἄνυδροι 'waterless clouds' [Alf, BNTC; KJV, NAB, NIV]: waterless clouds, (and they are) being carried along

QUESTION—What is implied by ὑπὸ ἀνέμων παραφερόμεναι 'being carried along by winds'?
    It refers to their lack of willpower [TG, TH].

late-autumn[a] trees, unfruitful,[b] twice[c] having-died,[d] having-been-uprooted,[e]

LEXICON—a. φθινοπωρινός (LN **67.164**) (BAGD p. 857): 'late autumn' [BAGD, BNTC, LN; TNT], 'autumn' [AB, Alf; ISV, NET, NIV, NJB, NRSV, REB, TEV], 'autumnal' [Lns, WBC], 'at harvest time' [NLT], 'at the year's end' [NAB], 'leafless' [CEV], 'whose fruit withereth' [KJV]. It refers to trees as they are in autumn, without fruit [Hu, Lg], to harvest time when fruit was to be expected [EGT, El, Lns, WBC]; it refers to the time of approaching winter [BNTC, ICC, Law, Lg] with tree branches bare of leaves [BNTC, ICC, Law] and growth almost stopped [BNTC, ICC], when no fruit was expected [BNTC].

b. ἄκαρπος (LN **23.202**) (BAGD 1. p. 29): 'unfruitful' [BAGD], 'fruitless' [AB, Lns; ISV, REB, TNT], 'bearing no fruit' [BNTC, LN, WBC], 'without fruit' [Alf, LN; KJV, NET, NIV, NLT, NRSV], 'that bear no fruit' [**LN**; TEV], 'they bear no fruit' [NAB], 'unable to produce fruit' [CEV], 'barren' [NJB], 'producing no harvest' [LN]. This word explains the preceding φθινοπωρινά 'late autumn' [Alf, Blm, BNTC]. It means not producing fruit [Hie, Law], without fruit at harvest-time [Lg, NIBC, TH; TEV], incapable of producing fruit [Lg(M)]. It carries further the thought that the false teachers have nothing to offer to their hearers [BNTC].

c. δίς (LN **23.123**, 60.69) (BAGD p. 199): 'twice' [Alf, BAGD, LN (60.69), Lns; ISV, KJV, NET, NIV, NJB, NRSV], 'twice over' [BNTC, WBC; REB], 'doubly' [AB; NLT, TNT]. The phrase δίς ἀποθανόντα 'twice having died' is translated 'to be dead' [NAB]; translated as an adjective: 'dead' [CEV]; as an adjectival phrase: 'completely dead' [LN (23.123); TEV].

d. aorist act. participle of ἀποθνῄσκω (LN 23.99) (BAGD 1.a.β. p. 91): 'to die' [BAGD, LN]. This participle is translated as an adjective: 'dead' [AB, Alf, BNTC, Lns, WBC; all versions except CEV, NAB, TEV].

e. aorist pass. participle of ἐκριζόω (LN 43.11) (BAGD 1. p. 245): 'to be uprooted' [AB, BAGD, BNTC, LN, WBC; CEV, ISV, NAB, NET, NIV, NJB, NRSV], 'to be rooted out' [Alf], 'to be pulled out by the roots' [LN; NLT], 'to be pulled up by the roots' [REB, TEV], 'to be plucked up by the roots' [Lns; KJV], 'torn up by the roots' [TNT]. The prefix ἐκ- is intensive and adds the idea of direction, 'out of' [NTC]. This word explains the preceding phrase δίς ἀποθανόντα 'twice having died' [Blm]. The aorist participle implies their certain future doom [BNTC]; it implies that God has already judged them [Hie]. It implies having been shaken loose by the roots but remaining in the earth, incapable of bearing fruit [Lg]. The passive voice implies God as the actor [NTC].

QUESTION—What is implied by this phrase?

It implies that the false teachers have nothing to offer to their hearers [BNTC, TH, TNTC]. Autumn is the time for trees to bear fruit, and if they do not have fruit by then, they are worthless [TG].

QUESTION—What is indicated by the nominative case adjective φθινοπωρινά 'late autumn'?

1. It describes a characteristic of the nominative noun δένδρα 'trees' [Alf; ISV, NIV, NJB, NRSV]: late-autumn-type trees
2. It is translated as if it were in the dative case, stating the time of year [AB, BAGD, Hu, LN; NAB, NLT, REB, TEV, TNT]: trees in late autumn.

JUDE 1:12

QUESTION—What is meant by the participial phrase δὶς ἀποθανόντα 'twice having died'?

This phrase means utterly dead [El], dead and dried up [Hu], dead in appearance and dead in reality [Alf], without fruit and uprooted [EBC, NTC; NIV, NJB, NLT], without natural sap and uprooted [EGT], dead because of their fruitlessness and therefore destroyed by the farmer [NIBC], symbolizing uselessness [NTC]; as applied to the false teachers, it means dead in themselves and uprooted [Lns], spiritually dead and destined for the second death at the Judgment [BNTC, Hie, TBST, WBC], once dead in sin, made alive in baptism, and then having become apostates and therefore twice dead [Lg(M), TNTC], born in sin, never regenerated, and doomed to eternal death [Law]. The condition already exists [TNTC].

1. It is probably attributive to δένδρα 'trees' [BNTC, Lns, WBC; all versions except NAB]: trees which have died twice.
2. It may be in predicate relation to δένδρα 'trees' [AB, Alf; NIV]: late autumn trees, (and they) have died twice.

QUESTION—What relationship is indicated by the participle ἐκριζωθέντα 'having been uprooted'?

They have not produced good works and are incapable of doing so in the future [Hu].

1. It is probably attributive to δένδρα 'trees' [BNTC, Lns, WBC; all versions except NAB, NLT]: trees which have been uprooted.
2. It expresses the result [Hu; NLT]: having died twice and as a result having been uprooted.
3. It may be in predicate relation to δένδρα 'trees' [AB, Alf; NAB]: late autumn trees, (and they) have been uprooted.

13 wild[a] waves of-(the)-sea foaming-up[b] their-own shames,[c]

LEXICON—a. ἄγριος (LN **20.6**) (BAGD 2. p. 13): 'wild' [AB, Alf, BNTC, Lns, WBC; all versions except KJV], 'stormy' [BAGD, **LN**], 'violent' [LN], 'raging' [KJV]. It means 'wild' in contrast to domesticated [Hie]. It implies lack of self-control [BNTC], being restless and unrestrained [Hie].

b. pres. act. participle of ἐπαφρίζω (LN **14.29**) (BAGD p. 284): 'to foam up' [Alf; NIV], 'to foam out' [Lns], 'to foam' [REB], 'to cast foam' [AB], 'to cast up like foam' [BAGD], 'to cast up the foam' [WBC; NRSV], 'to toss up' [TNT], 'to toss up as foam' [BNTC], 'to splash abroad like foam' [NAB], 'to foam out' [KJV], 'to spew out foam' [NET], 'to churn up the foam' [ISV], 'to churn up the dirty foam' [NLT], 'to show up like foam' [CEV, TEV], 'to cause to foam up' [LN]. The phrase ἐπαφρίζοντα τὰς ἑαυτῶν αἰσχύνας 'foaming up their own shames' is translated 'with their own shame for foam' [NJB]. It refers to foaming up onto the shore [Blm, Hie, NIBC, TH]. The present tense implies continual conduct [Law].

c. αἰσχύνη (LN 25.191, **88.149**) (BAGD 3. p. 25): 'shame' [AB, Alf, Lns; ISV, KJV, NET, NIV, NJB, NRSV], 'shameful deed' [BAGD, BNTC, LN (88.149); CEV, NLT, TEV], 'shameless deed' [NAB, TNT], 'disgraceful deed' [REB], 'that which causes shame' [LN (25.191)], 'abomination' [WBC]. It refers to shameful acts [El, TNTC; NET] or shameful words [NET]. The plural here refers to the various forms of their shameful actions [Law, Lg]. It refers to the shameful nature of the false teachers [Hu].

QUESTION—How are the two nouns related in the genitive phrase κύματα ἄγρια θαλάσσης 'wild waves of the sea'?

The genitive noun θαλάσσης 'sea' describes κύματα ἄγρια 'wild waves' [NAB, NET]: wild sea waves. The phrase implies that these persons are restless and untamed [Law, NIBC, NTC]; they resist divine orders and are impure and hurtful [Lg]; they spread their teachings and bring confusion to Christians [TH].

QUESTION—What relationship is indicated by the participle ἐπαφρίζοντα 'foaming up'?
1. It is attributive [AB]: wild waves who foam up.
2. It is intensive and causative [NET]: waves causing foam.
3. It is probably a predicate nominative: wild waves, (and they) foam up.

QUESTION—What relationship is indicated by the accusative τὰς ἑαυτῶν αἰσχύνας 'their own shames'?
1. It is the direct object of the verb [Alf, EGT, Lns; KJV, NAB, NIV, TNT]: waves foaming up their shames. It refers to refuse thrown onto the beach by the waves [EGT, Hie, Law, Lns, NIBC, NTC, TBST, TH, WBC]. The shameful deeds show up on the waves [CEV, REB, TEV]; the shameful deeds are the foam of the waves [BNTC, EBC, WBC; NJB]
2. It receives the action of the verb [AB]: cast foam over their own shames.
3. The shames are related to the foam [ISV, NLT, NRSV]: the waves churn up the foam of the shames.

stars wanderers[a] for-whom the gloom[b] of-the darkness[c] into[d] (the) age is-kept.[e]

LEXICON—a. πλανήτης (LN **15.26**) (BAGD p. 666): 'wanderer' [LN]. This noun is translated as a participle: 'wandering' [AB, Alf, BAGD, **LN**, Lns, WBC; all versions except NAB, NET, REB], 'shooting' [NAB], 'wayward' [NET]; as a phrase: 'that have wandered from their courses' [REB], 'straying from their courses' [BNTC]. This word is an adjective [BNTC].

b. ζόφος (LN **1.24**, 14.57) (BAGD 2. p. 339): 'gloom' [LN; NJB, NLT], 'thick gloom' [NAB], 'murky gloom' [BNTC], 'nether gloom' [WBC], 'blackness' [Alf, Lns; KJV], 'black utter depths' [NET], 'darkness' [LN], 'darkest pits' [CEV]. This noun is also translated as an adjective: 'blackest' [NIV, REB, TNT], 'deepest' [ISV, NRSV, TEV], 'gloomy' [AB, BAGD]. The phrase ὁ ζόφος τοῦ σκότους 'the gloom of the darkness' is translated 'the black darkness' [BAGD], 'gloomy hell' [BAGD], 'the darkness of hell' [**LN**].

c. σκότος (LN 14.53, 88.125) (BAGD 1. p. 757): 'darkness' [AB, Alf, BAGD, BNTC, LN (14.53, 88.125), Lns, WBC; all versions except CEV, TNT], 'the place of darkness' [TNT], 'gloom' [BAGD], 'sin' [LN (88.125)], 'hell' [CEV].

d. εἰς with accusative object (LN **67.95**, 84.22): 'into' [LN (84.22)]. The phrase εἰς αἰῶνα 'into the age' is translated 'forever' [AB, Alf, BNTC, LN (67.95), Lns, WBC; all versions except NLT, REB], 'everlasting' [NLT], 'eternal' [NET]. This phrase emphasizes the eternal extent of the punishment [Law] and emphasizes the concept of the following verb 'held' [Hie].

e. perf. pass. indicative of τηρέω (LN 13.32) (BAGD 2.a. p. 815): 'to be kept' [AB, BAGD, LN, Lns], 'to be held' [BAGD], 'to be reserved' [Alf, BAGD, BNTC, WBC; ISV, KJV, NAB, NET, NIV, NRSV, REB, TNT], 'to be stored up' [NJB], 'to be retained' [LN], 'to be doomed' [CEV]. The phrase οἷς ... τετήρηται is translated 'to head for' [NLT]. The perfect tense indicates fixedness and finality [Hie]. The passive voice implies God as the actor [NTC, TG, TH].

QUESTION—What relationship is indicated by the phrase ἀστέρες πλανῆται 'stars wanderers'?

These two nouns are in apposition with one another [NTC]: stars that are planets. The application is to professing Christian teachers (these persons are not authorized teachers [Lg]) who drift about in instability [Alf, Law, Lg(M)] and in false doctrines and practice [Alf, Lg(M)], who profess to give guidance but instead lead people astray [TBST], who had wandered from the truth [NIBC, TNTC, WBC] because of rebelling against God [NIBC], rejecting God's government [Law], in order to entice others to sin [WBC]; instead, they bring confusion and loss to their hearers [Hie]. It refers to the unsettled habits of the teachers [Blm], to people who have abandoned their true faith [CBC], who use God's grace as an excuse for immoral living [EGT].

1. The figure refers to the planets [BNTC, CBC, EBC, ICC, Lns, NIBC, NTC, TBST, TH], which the ancient people thought moved irregularly [BNTC, CBC, NIBC, TH].

2. The figure refers to comets [Alf, Hie, Hu, Lg(M)], meteors [Hie], shooting stars [TNTC; NAB].

3. The figure refers to wandering stars [all versions except NAB] which leave their proper place and wander away [El, Lg, TG; NET, REB], stars which have no fixed place in the heavens [Law]. Since the stars are not fixed, they are unreliable and give disastrous guidance [NET].

QUESTION—To what does οἷς 'for whom' refer?

1. It refers to ἀστέρες πλανῆται 'wandering stars' [AB, Alf, BNTC, WBC; all versions except possibly REB]: wandering stars, for whom ...

2. It refers back to οὗτοι 'these persons' in verse 12 [Hu, Lns, NTC]: these persons, for whom ...

QUESTION—How are the two nouns related in the genitive phrase ὁ ζόφος τοῦ σκότους 'the gloom of the darkness'?
1. They are translated as two concepts [NLT]: gloom and darkness.
2. It is one concept [AB, CBC, Law, NIBC, NTC, TG, TH; CEV, ISV, NET, NIV, NRSV, REB, TEV, TNT]. The double designation intensifies the description [Hie, Hu, Lns, NIBC; ISV, NRSV, REB, TEV, TNT]. It is a Hebraistic expression implying exceedingly great darkness, farthest from God [Law]. It refers to the place of future punishment [TH]. It refers to the depths of Sheol, as in verse 6 [TG].

QUESTION—What is the phrase εἰς αἰῶνα 'into the age' connected with?
1. It is connected with τετήρηται 'is kept' [AB, Alf, BNTC, Hie, NTC, WBC; CEV, ISV, NAB, NIV, NJB, NRSV, TNT]: is kept forever.
2. It is connected with ὁ ζόφος τοῦ σκότους 'the gloom of the darkness' [EBC, Lns; NET, NLT, REB]: the eternal gloom of the darkness.

DISCOURSE UNIT: 14–16 [AB, BNTC, EBC, EGT, Law, Lns, TBST, TNTC, WBC]. The topic is a prediction of future judgment [AB], Enoch's prophecy [BNTC, EGT, Lns, TNTC, WBC], Enoch's prophecy of the coming judgment [EBC], the coming revelation of Christ and the apostates [Law], a further warning example of judgment [TBST].

DISCOURSE UNIT: 14–15 [Hie]. The topic is the prophecy of the apostates' doom.

14 **And with-respect-to/to-these-persons also prophesied Enoch, seventh from^a Adam, saying,**

LEXICON—a. ἀπό with genitive object (LN 67.131): 'from' [AB, Alf, BNTC, LN, Lns; ISV, KJV, NIV, NJB, NRSV], 'since' [LN], 'after' [CEV, NLT], 'descended from' [NAB], 'direct descendant from' [TEV], 'in descent from' [WBC; REB], 'in line from' [TNT], 'beginning with' [NET].

QUESTION—What relationship is indicated by δέ 'and'?
It introduces a further aspect [Hie, Lns; NET] but different from the preceding subject [Hie; NET].

QUESTION—What relationship is indicated by προεφήτευσεν 'prophesied' as the first word in the Greek sentence?
1. Concerning the word order.
1.1 It is emphatic, indicating the importance of the prophecy [Hie, Law].
1.2 It is the normal position for the principal verb [Editor].
2. Concerning the use of this word.
2.1 It does not imply that the quotation is inspired prophecy [Blm, NTC].
2.2 It implies that the author regarded the book of Enoch as the work of the biblical Enoch and therefore inspired [BNTC].

JUDE 1:14

QUESTION—What relationship is indicated by the reference to ἕβδομος 'seventh'?

The biblical Enoch was the seventh generation from Adam (including Adam as the first generation by Hebrew reckoning) [BNTC, EBC, EGT, Hie, Lg, Lns, NIBC, NTC, TBST, TG, TH, WBC; NET]. So Enoch was the sixth direct descendant from Adam [TG; NET]. 'Seven' as a sacred (perfect [TH]) number implying completeness marks the importance of Enoch (of Enoch's prophecy [TH]) [BNTC, Hu, Lg(M), NIBC, NTC, TH, TNTC, WBC]. It may also imply the great antiquity of the prophecy [Hie]. It merely identifies the Enoch referred to [Lns, TBST].

QUESTION—What relationship is indicated by the dative τούτοις 'these'?

1. It is a dative of reference [Alf, BNTC, Hu, Law, Lg, TBST, WBC; all versions]: he prophesied with reference to these persons. It refers to the false teachers of Jude's day [TBST, TNTC, WBC]; Jude is applying the prophecy to the false teachers of his day [EGT]. It indicates a negative reference, prophesying against them [REB].
2. It is a dative of disadvantage [NET]: he prophesied against them.
3. It is an indirect object, referring to the persons before the Flood, meaning that Enoch prophesied to those persons and Jude is applying the prophecy to the false teachers of his day [Blm, Hie, ICC]: he prophesied to these also.

QUESTION—What relationship is indicated by καί 'also'?

1. It is related to τούτοις 'these persons' [Hie, Lns] according to normal Greek word order: to these persons also. It means for these false teachers as well as for the wicked people of Enoch's time [Lns].
2. It refers to προεφήτευσεν 'prophesied' [BNTC, Lg], with καί 'also' displaced from its normal position [BNTC]: he too prophesied.
3. The words δὲ καί 'and also' are to be taken together, applying to the whole verse [Alf]: yes, and . . .

QUESTION—What relationship is indicated by the participle λέγων 'saying'?

1. It is in apposition with προεφήτευσεν 'prophesied', restating the concept with another word [Editor]: he prophesied, i.e., he said.
2. It is temporal [ISV, NAB, NJB, REB, TNT]: when he said.
3. It is translated as a separate proposition [NLT]: he said.

QUESTION—What is implied by this reference to 'Enoch, seventh from Adam'?

1. It means that Jude is quoting from the apocryphal book of Enoch [Blm, EBC, Hie, ICC, TBST, TH, TNTC] as a true statement [EBC, Hie], without implying that he accepted it as inspired scripture [Blm, EBC, Hie, NIBC, NTC]. However, Jude's use of the quotation is inspired and authoritative [NTC].
2. It means that Jude regarded the prophecy he quotes as inspired by God, but not necessarily that the book of Enoch is canonical [WBC].

JUDE 1:14 57

3. It means that Jude quoted the biblical Enoch [Law, Lg, Lns], not the apocryphal book of Enoch [Law]; this is supported by the addition of the phrase ἕβδομος ἀπὸ Ἀδάμ 'seventh from Adam' [Law].

"Behold, (the) Lord came with[a] his holy[b] myriads[c]

TEXT—Instead of ἁγίαις μυριάσιν 'holy myriads', some manuscripts read ἁγίαις μυριάσιν ἀγγέλων 'holy myriads of angels', and other manuscripts read μυριάσιν ἁγίων ἀγγέλων 'myriads of holy angels'. GNT does not deal with this variant. 'Myriads of holy angels' is read by CEV, TEV, and 'myriads of angels' is read by REB; but the addition of 'angels' is probably editorial rather than based on the textual addition of this word.

LEXICON—a. ἐν with dative object (LN 89.119) (BAGD I.4.c.α. p. 259): 'with' [AB, BAGD, BNTC, LN, WBC; all versions], 'among' [Alf], 'in union with' [LN], 'in connection with' [Lns]. It means 'surrounded by' [Alf, El, Hie, Law]; it means 'to be glorified in them' [Lg].

b. ἅγιος (LN 88.24) (BAGD 1.b.β. p. 9): 'holy' [AB, Alf, BAGD, BNTC, LN, Lns, WBC; all versions except KJV, NET, REB], 'holy ones' [NET], 'saint' [KJV], 'angel' [REB].

c. μυριάς (LN 60.8, 60.45) (BAGD 2. p. 529): 'myriad' [Alf, BAGD, BNTC, Lns; REB], 'great host' [TNT], 'innumerable' [LN (60.8)], 'countless' [LN (60.8); NAB], 'thousands' [NLT], 'many thousands' [TEV], 'countless thousands' [ISV], 'thousands and thousands' [CEV, NET], 'thousands upon thousands' [NIV], 'ten thousand' [LN (60.45)], 'ten thousands' [KJV, NRSV], 'tens of thousands' [AB, WBC; NJB].

QUESTION—What relationship is indicated by ἰδού 'behold'?

It calls special attention to the following prophecy [Hie].

QUESTION—To whom does κύριος 'Lord' refer?

It refers to Jesus [TH] in his second coming [Hie, NTC].

QUESTION—What is the meaning of the aorist tense of ἦλθεν 'he came'?

1. It refers to the future [NIBC, NTC; NJB, TEV] as a prophetic aorist [Alf, EGT, Hie, Law, Lg(M), Lns, NIBC, NTC, TH], a Semitic prophetic perfect [AB, WBC]: he will come. It refers to the second coming of Christ [EBC, NIBC, TNTC, WBC]. This use of the aorist tense emphasizes the certainty of the future event [Hie, Law, TH].
2. It is translated 'he is coming' [AB; CEV, KJV, NET, NIV, NLT, NRSV].
3. It is translated as past time [BNTC, Lns, WBC; ISV, NAB, NET, REB, TNT]: he has come. The phrase ἰδοὺ ἦλθεν κύριος 'behold, the Lord came' is translated 'I saw the Lord come' [REB].

QUESTION—To whom does ἁγίαις μυριάσιν αὐτοῦ 'his holy myriads' refer?

1. It refers to 'holy ones' [AB, NIBC, NTC, TNTC, WBC; ISV, NAB, NET, NIV, NJB, NLT, NRSV, TNT]. They are angels [AB, Alf, Hie, Lns, NIBC, NTC, TH, TNTC, WBC; CEV, REB, TEV]. The genitive pronoun αὐτοῦ 'his' implies that the 'holy myriads' belong to Jesus and serve him [Hie, Lg]. Ἁγίαις 'holy' refers to their moral character [Hie]; it means that they are dedicated servants of God [TH].

2. It refers to saints [KJV].

15 to-do^a judgment^b against^c all (persons)

LEXICON—a. aorist act. infin. of ποιέω (LN 42.7, 90.45) (BAGD I.1.b.δ. p. 681): 'to do' [BAGD, LN (42.7, 90.45)], 'to bring' [TEV, TNT], 'to bring to' [REB], 'to carry out' [LN (42.7)], 'to accomplish' [BAGD, LN (42.7)], 'to execute' [Alf, BNTC, Lns, WBC; ISV, KJV, NET, NRSV], 'to pass' [AB; NAB], 'to pronounce' [NJB], 'to bring to' [NLT], not explicit [CEV, NIV].

b. κρίσις (LN 38.1, 56.24, 56.30) (BAGD 1.a.β. p. 452): 'judgment' [AB, Alf, BAGD, BNTC, LN (56.24), WBC; all versions except CEV, NIV], 'judging down' [Lns], 'condemnation' [LN (56.30)], 'punishment' [LN (38.1)]. This noun is also translated as a verb: 'to judge' [CEV, NIV]. It refers to examining the evidence and pronouncing the resultant verdict [Hie], the punishment applied [Law]. It implies condemnation [BNTC].

c. κατά with genitive object (LN 90.31) (BAGD I.2.b.β. p. 405): 'against' [BAGD, LN], 'on' [AB, BNTC, Lns, WBC; ISV, NAB, NET, NJB, NRSV, TEV], 'upon' [Alf; KJV]. The phrase κατὰ πάντων 'against all persons' is translated 'universal' [TNT]. It implies a verdict of condemnation [Hie].

QUESTION—What relationship is indicated by the infinitive ποιῆσαι 'to do'?

1. It express purpose [Law]: for the purpose of doing judgment.
2. It is translated as an independent statement [ISV]: he will do judgment.

QUESTION—To whom does κατὰ πάντων 'against all' refer?

1. It includes everyone [Hie, Lns, TH; all versions].
2. It refers to all the wicked [BNTC, Law, NIBC, WBC]

and to-convict^a every person^b concerning^c all their deeds^d of-impiety^e which they-have-done-impiously^f

TEXT—Instead of πᾶσαν ψυχήν 'every soul', some manuscripts read πάντας τοὺς ἀσεβεῖς 'all the ungodly' and some read πάντας τοὺς ἀσεβεῖς αὐτῶν 'all the ungodly of them'. GNT does not deal with this variant. Πᾶσαν ψυχήν 'every soul' is read by ISV, NET, NRSV, TEV; πάντας τοὺς ἀσεβεῖς 'all the ungodly' is read by AB, Alf, BNTC, EGT, El, Hie, Law, Lns, NIBC, NTC, TBST, WBC, CEV, NAB, NIV, NJB, NLT, REB, TNT; πάντας τοὺς ἀσεβεῖς αὐτῶν 'all the ungodly of them' is read by Blm, KJV, Lg(M).

LEXICON—a. aorist act. infin. of ἐλέγχω (LN 33.417) (BAGD 2. p. 249): 'to convict' [AB, Alf, BAGD, BNTC, Lns, WBC; ISV, NAB, NET, NIV, NLT, NRSV, REB, TNT], 'to indict' [NAB], 'to convince' [BAGD; KJV], 'to punish' [CEV], 'to sentence' [NJB], 'to condemn' [TEV], 'to rebuke' [LN]. It means to convict [Law]; it includes establishing guilt [Hie].

b. ψυχή (LN 9.20): 'person' [LN; NET]. The phrase πᾶσαν ψυχήν 'every person' is translated 'everyone' [ISV, NRSV], 'them' [TEV]. Different text: 'ungodly people' [CEV], 'ungodly ones' [TNT], 'ungodly' [AB,

BNTC, Lns, WBC; NIV, NLT], 'godless' [NAB, NJB, REB], 'impious' [Alf], 'ungodly of them' [KJV].
c. περί with genitive object (LN 89.6, 90.24): 'concerning' [Alf, LN (89.6, 90.24), Lns], 'about' [LN (90.24)], 'with regard to' [LN (89.6)], 'for' [CEV, NAB, NJB, TEV], 'of' [AB, BNTC, WBC; ISV, KJV, NET, NIV, NLT, NRSV, REB, TNT].
d. ἔργον (LN 42.11) (BAGD 1.c.β. p. 308): 'deed' [AB, BAGD, BNTC, LN, WBC; KJV, NAB, NET, NRSV, REB, TEV, TNT], 'work' [Alf, Lns], 'act' [LN; NIV], 'thing' [CEV, ISV, NJB, NLT].
e. ἀσέβεια (LN **53.10**) (BAGD p. 114): 'impiety' [Alf, BAGD], 'godlessness' [BAGD, **LN**], 'ungodliness' [BNTC, Lns; NRSV]. This genitive noun is translated as a phrase: 'without any regard for God' [**LN**], 'when they acted in a godless way' [**LN**]; as an adjective: 'godless' [AB; NJB, REB, TEV], 'ungodly' [WBC; ISV, KJV, NET, NIV, TNT], 'evil' [CEV, NAB, NLT]. It refers to lack of reverence toward God [Law]. The repeated use in this verse of words related to ἀσέβεια 'impiety' adds emphasis to the description of the false teachers [BNTC, Hie, Hu, TH], to the seriousness of the false teachers' sins [NTC, TH], to the certainty of their judgment [NIBC], to how widespread is their influence [TBST].
f. aorist act. indic. of ἀσεβέω (LN **53.10**) (BAGD p. 114): 'to do impiously' [Alf], 'to do godlessly' [AB], 'to do in the ungodly way' [NIV], 'to do in such an ungodly way' [ISV], 'to do ungodlywise' [Lns], 'to do (ungodly deeds)' [CEV, NAB, NJB], 'to do (evil things) in rebellion' [NLT], 'to do (deeds) by ungodly living' [LN], 'to commit impious deeds' [BAGD], 'to commit ungodly' [KJV], 'to commit in such an ungodly way' [NRSV], 'to commit in ungodliness' [WBC], 'to commit (godless deeds)' [BNTC; REB], 'to perform (godless deeds)' [TEV], not explicit [TNT]. The phrase 'all their deeds of impiety which they have done impiously' is translated 'all their thoroughly ungodly deeds that they have committed' [NET]. The word implies acting out of their ungodly nature [Hie].

QUESTION—What relationship is indicated by the infinitive ἐλέγξαι 'to reprove'?
1. It expresses purpose [Law]: in order to reprove.
2. It is translated as a separate statement [CEV, NLT] parallel to ποιῆσαι κρίσιν 'to do judgment' [ISV]: he will do judgment and will reprove.

QUESTION—What relationship is indicated by the repeated use of forms of πᾶς 'all'?
It indicates that this concept is important [EBC, NTC, TBST], stressing the universality of the judgment [Hie].

QUESTION—How are the two nouns related in the genitive construction ἔργων ἀσεβείας 'deeds of impiety'?
Ἀσεβείας 'impiety' is qualitative, describing ἔργων 'deeds' [AB, WBC; all versions]: impious deeds.

and concerning^a all the hard^b (things) which they-have-spoken^c against^d him, impious^e sinners."

LEXICON—a. περί with genitive object: 'concerning'. See this word above.

    b. σκληρός (LN **88.135**) (BAGD 1.b. p. 756): 'hard' [Alf, BAGD, Lns, WBC; KJV], 'harsh' [BAGD, LN; ISV, NAB, NET, NIV, NRSV, TNT], 'defiant' [AB; NJB, REB], 'despiteful' [BNTC], 'evil' [CEV], 'terrible' [TEV]. This adjective is translated as a substantive: 'insult' [NLT]. It refers to words [TH]. It means harsh [El, Hie], offensive [Hie], ungodly [Hu], defiant [TH], impious blasphemy [Lg].

    c. aorist act. indic. of λαλέω (LN 33.70): 'to speak' [AB, Alf, BNTC, LN, WBC; KJV, NET, NIV, NLT, NRSV, REB, TEV], 'to say' [LN, Lns; CEV, ISV, TNT], 'to utter' [NAB]. This active verb is translated as a passive, with 'impious sinners' as subject: 'to be said' [NJB].

    d. κατά with genitive object: (LN 90.31) (BAGD I.2.b.β. p. 405): 'against' [AB, Alf, BAGD, BNTC, LN, Lns, WBC; all versions except CEV, ISV], 'about' [CEV, ISV].

    e. ἀσεβής (LN 53.11) (BAGD 1. p. 114): 'impious' [Alf, BAGD], 'godless' [AB, BAGD; NAB, NJB, NLT, REB, TEV, TNT], 'ungodly' [BNTC, LN, Lns, WBC; CEV, ISV, KJV, NET, NIV, NRSV].

QUESTION—To whom does the phrase κατ' αὐτοῦ 'against him' refer?

    1. It refers to Christ [Hie].

    2. It refers to God [TH].

QUESTION—What relationship is indicated by the nominative phrase ἁμαρτωλοὶ ἀσεβεῖς 'impious sinners'?

    It is emphatic by its final position [Hie, Hu, NTC].

    1. It is the subject of the verb ἐλάλησαν 'spoke' [AB, Alf, WBC; all versions except REB, TNT]: impious sinners spoke.

    2. It is in apposition with the understood subject of ἐλάλησαν 'spoke' [BNTC, Hie, Lns; REB, TNT]: they spoke, impious sinners.

DISCOURSE UNIT: 16–23 [Lg]. The topic is a further description of the false teachers, and an exhortation to the believers.

DISCOURSE UNIT: 16 [Hie]. The topic is a summary description of the false teachers.

16 These (persons) are grumblers,^a complaining,^b

LEXICON—a. γογγυστής (LN **33.386**) (BAGD p. 164): 'grumbler' [BAGD, BNTC, **LN**; NAB, NET, NIV, NJB, NLT, NRSV, REB], 'complainer' [LN; ISV], 'murmurer' [Alf, Lns, WBC; KJV]. This noun is translated as an adjective: 'disgruntled' [AB]; as a verb: 'to grumble' [CEV, TEV, TNT]. It refers to discontent expressed in muttered undertones [Hie, Law], discontented complaining [Law]. It is a general term [Hie] referring to inward expression [Lg], referring to their view of God [Lg(M)], referring to grumbling against God [ICC, NTC, TH, TNTC] and the restrictions of God's law [TNTC], and against the authority figures [ICC], against the authority of God or Christ [WBC], Christians grumbling about conditions on earth [TBST].

b. μεμψίμοιρος (LN **33.432**) (BAGD p. 502): 'complaining' [BAGD], 'constantly blaming' [**LN**], 'fault-finding' [BAGD, LN], 'discontented' [WBC]. This adjective is translated as a noun: 'complainer' [Lns; KJV, NLT], 'faultfinder' [ISV, NET, NIV], 'whiner' [NAB], 'malcontent' [NRSV, REB], 'mischief-maker' [NJB], 'murmurer' [AB]; as a verb: 'to complain' [CEV, TNT], 'to complain of one's lot' [BNTC], 'to blame others' [TEV], 'to be dissatisfied with one's lot' [Alf]. It means to blame one's fate [BNTC]; it refers to critical complaining [EBC], grumbling against authority [ICC], dissatisfaction with one's lot [Hu, Law, Lg, NIBC, TBST, TH, TNTC, WBC], finding fault with God [Lg], blaming others for their lot [TH], envying non-Christians' way of life [TBST], desiring to reject the moral restrictions of God's law [WBC], outward feelings [Lg]. This word is more specific than the preceding word [Hie, Hu]; it is synonymous with the preceding word [NTC].

QUESTION—What is the function of this phrase?

It is a further description of the false teachers [Hu]. It describes the false teachers' rude complaining attitude toward God [BNTC], against church authority [CBC]. This and the following phrase deal with the false teachers' reaction to affairs of life [Hie]. The opening words οὗτοί εἰσιν 'these persons are' add emphasis [Hu]; they refer to the same people as in verse 15 [TH].

going[a] according-to[b] their-own desires,[c]

LEXICON—a. pres. mid. (deponent = act.) participle of πορεύω (πορεύομαι LN 15.10, 41.11) (BAGD 2.c. p. 692): 'to go' [AB, LN (15.10); NET], 'to proceed' [Lns], 'to walk' [Alf, BAGD; KJV], 'to follow' [BNTC, WBC; ISV, NIV, REB, TEV], 'to live' [BAGD, LN (41.11); CEV, NAB, TNT], 'to behave' [LN (41.11)], 'to conduct oneself' [BAGD], 'to do' [NLT], 'to go about doing' [LN (41.11)], 'to indulge' [NRSV]. This deponent verb is translated as a passive: 'to be governed' [NJB].

b. κατά with accusative object (LN 89.8): 'according to' [Alf, Lns], 'by' [CEV, NAB, NJB], 'in accordance with' [LN], 'after' [KJV], 'for' [TNT], 'the way of' [AB], not explicit [BNTC, WBC; ISV, NET, NIV, NLT, NRSV, REB, TEV].

c. ἐπιθυμία (LN 25.12) (BAGD 3. p. 293): 'desire' [BAGD, BNTC, LN, WBC; ISV, NET, NJB], 'selfish desire' [CEV, TNT], 'evil desire' [NIV, TEV], 'passion' [AB; NAB], 'lust' [Alf, Lns; KJV, NRSV, REB], 'whatever evil they feel like' [NLT]. It refers to physical lusts [NTC].

QUESTION—What is the function of this participial phrase?

It implies following their own (selfish [CEV, TNT]) (evil [Hie, TBST, TH, TNTC, WBC; NIV, NLT, TEV]) desires [Alf, Blm, BNTC, EBC, EGT, Hie, Hu, Law, Lns, NIBC, TBST, TH, TNTC, WBC; all versions] rather than seeking God's will [Blm, EGT, Hie, NIBC, WBC], a rebellious attitude against church authorities [CBC]. It refers to dissatisfaction and complaining about one's lot in life [Hie], complaining because their lusts are not satisfied [Lns]. The present tense implies a habitual way of life [Law].

QUESTION—What is this participial phrase connected with?
1. It is independent [CEV, NAB, NIV, NRSV, REB, TEV, TNT]: they go according to their own desires.
2. It is connected with the phrase γογγυσταί μεμψίμοιροι 'grumblers, complainers' [AB, Alf, BNTC, Lns, WBC; ISV, KJV, NLT]: grumblers, complainers, going according to their own desires.
3. It is connected only with μεμψίμοιροι 'complainers' [NJB]: they are grumblers; they are complainers going according to their own desires.

QUESTION—What relationship is indicated by the participle πορευόμενοι 'going'?
1. It is attributive [AB, BNTC, WBC; NET]: grumblers and complainers who go.
2. It is translated as an independent action [CEV, NAB, NIV, NRSV, REB, TEV, TNT]: grumblers, complainers; they go.

and their mouth speaks haughty[a] (words),

LEXICON—a. ὑπέρογκος (LN 33.373) (BAGD p. 841): 'haughty' [BAGD], 'arrogant' [ISV, WBC], 'bombastic' [BAGD, BNTC; NRSV], 'boastful' [LN; NJB], 'grandiose' [Lns], 'great swelling' [Alf; KJV]. This adjective is translated as a noun: 'bombast' [NAB, REB]; as an adverb: 'inflatedly' [AB], 'arrogantly' [TNT]. This entire phrase is translated 'they brag about themselves' [CEV, TEV], 'they boast about themselves' [NIV], 'they are loudmouthed braggarts' [NLT], 'they give bombastic speeches' [NET]. It refers to bombastic words about themselves [TNTC], haughty [Law, NTC], self-exalting words [Hu, Lg, NTC, TBST] actually uttered against God [TBST, WBC], arrogant talk against God [TH, WBC], arrogantly expressed false teachings about God [BNTC, Hie], rejection of God's moral authority [WBC], boastful words against church authorities [CBC].

QUESTION—What is the function of this clause?
1. This and the following phrase refer to the false teachers' relationships to other persons [Hie]. They speak bombastically in order to impress people [NIBC].
2. It is a parenthesis [BNTC].

QUESTION—What is implied by the reference to 'the mouth' speaking?
It calls attention to the bombastic nature of their public utterances [Hie].

wondering-at[a] faces[b] for-the-sake-of[c] benefit.[d]

LEXICON—a. pres. act. participle of θαυμάζω (LN 33.365) (BAGD 1.b.α. p. 352): 'to wonder at' [BAGD], 'to admire' [Alf, BAGD], 'to have in admiration' [KJV], 'to flatter' [BNTC, LN, Lns; CEV, ISV, NIV, NJB, NLT, NRSV, TEV], 'to fawn upon' [TNT]. (See b. for AB, WBC; NAB, NET, REB.)

b. πρόσωπον (LN 9.9) (BAGD 1.b. p. 721): 'face', 'person' [LN], 'other (person)' [CEV, NIV, NJB, NLT, TEV, TNT], '(a) man's person' [Alf; KJV], 'individual' [BNTC, LN]; this plural noun is translated 'people' [ISV, NRSV]; not explicit [Lns]. The phrase θαυμάζοντες πρόσωπα 'wondering at faces' is translated 'to flatter' [BAGD], 'to resort to flattery' [NAB], 'to court favor' [REB], 'to show partiality' [AB, WBC], 'to enchant folks' [NET].
c. χάριν with genitive object (LN 89.29, 89.60) (BAGD 1. p. 877): 'for the sake of' [Alf, BAGD, BNTC, LN (89.60), Lns, WBC], 'for the purpose of' [LN (89.60)], 'for' [AB; NET, NJB], 'because of' [LN (89.29); KJV], 'by reason of' [LN (89.29)].
d. ὠφέλεια (LN 65.41) (BAGD p. 900): 'benefit' [LN], 'advantage' [Alf, BAGD, BNTC, LN; KJV], 'gain' [AB, WBC; NJB], 'profit' [Lns]. The phrase ὠφελείας χάριν 'for the sake of benefit' is translated 'to get what they want' [CEV], 'to gain their ends' [REB], 'in order to get their own way' [TEV], 'to get favors in return' [NLT], 'to their own advantage' [NRSV], 'for their own advantage' [NIV], 'for their own gain' [NET], 'in order to take advantage of them' [ISV], 'if anything is to be gained by it' [TNT], 'whenever it is expedient' [NAB].

QUESTION—What is the meaning of this phrase?
It refers to showing partiality or flattery for the sake of gaining an advantage [Law, Lns, NIBC, NTC, TH, TNTC], teaching an erroneous message in order to win followers and gain influence [TBST, WBC]. It refers to sensuality [Lg]; it does not refer to sensuality [Lg(M)].

QUESTION—What relationship is indicated by the participle θαυμάζοντες 'wondering at'?
It is translated as an independent action [AB, BNTC, WBC; CEV, NIV, NLT, REB, TEV, TNT]: they flatter.

DISCOURSE UNIT: 17–23 [AB, BNTC, EBC, GNT, Hie, Lns, NTC, TG; CEV, ISV, NIV, NLT, TEV]. The topic is faithless false teachers and faithful disciples [AB], a call to remain faithful [NIV, NLT], exhortation to the faithful believers [BNTC, EBC, Hie, Lns, NTC] in the midst of apostasy [Hie], exhortation to Christian living [TG], warnings and exhortations [GNT], warnings and instructions [TEV], more warnings [CEV], advice to the readers [ISV].

DISCOURSE UNIT: 17–19 [EGT, Hie, Law, TBST, TNTC, WBC; NJB]. The topic is a warning [NJB], a reminder of the apostles' warnings [EGT, Law, TBST], the apostles' warnings apply to the readers [TNTC], an exhortation to beware of apostasy [Hie], the apostles' prophecy [WBC].

17 But you, beloved,[a] remember[b] the words[c] the-(ones) spoken-beforehand[d] by[e] the apostles of our Lord Jesus Christ

LEXICON—a. ἀγαπητός (LN 25.45) (BAGD 2. p. 6): 'beloved' [AB, Alf, LN, Lns; KJV, NAB, NRSV], 'dear friend' [BAGD, BNTC, WBC; CEV, ISV, NET, NIV, NJB, NLT, TNT], 'friend' [REB, TEV]. This word is a word

of tenderness [NTC], indicating the author's continuing personal affection for his readers [Hie].
b. aorist pass. (deponent = act.) impera. of μιμνῄσκομαι (LN 29.7, 29.16) (BAGD 1.a.α. p. 522): 'to remember' [AB, Alf, BAGD, BNTC, LN (29.7, 29.16), Lns, WBC; all versions], 'to recall' [LN (29.7); NET], 'to keep in mind' [BAGD]. It implies that the quotation which follows was well-known to the readers [El, Hu, Law, TH], not something new they were to commit to memory [TH]. The aorist imperative implies urgency [Hie, NTC], necessity [Law].
c. ῥῆμα (LN 33.9, 33.98) (BAGD 1. p. 735): 'word' [Alf, BAGD, BNTC, LN (33.9, 33.98), Lns; KJV], 'saying' [BAGD, LN (33.9, 33.98)], 'that which is said' [BAGD], 'statement, message' [LN (33.98)]. The phrase τῶν ῥημάτων τῶν προειρημένων 'the words the ones spoken beforehand' is translated 'the predictions' [REB], 'the predictions foretold' [NET], 'the warning you were given' [CEV], 'what you were told in the past' [TEV], 'what (they) foretold' [NIV, NJB], 'what (they) told you' [NLT]. The phrase τῶν ῥημάτων τῶν προειρημένων ὑπό 'the words the ones spoken beforehand by' is translated 'the predictions of' [WBC; NRSV], 'the statements and predictions of' [ISV], 'the prophetic words of' [NAB]. The phrase τῶν ῥημάτων τῶν προειρημένων ὑπὸ τῶν ἀποστόλων τοῦ κυρίου ἡμῶν Ἰησοῦ Χριστοῦ 'the words the ones spoken beforehand by the apostles of our Lord Jesus Christ' is translated 'what our Lord Jesus Christ said through his apostles' [TNT], 'what the apostles of our Lord Jesus Christ foretold' [AB]. Τῶν ῥημάτων 'these words' implies that the following quotation is a summary of what the apostles had taught [WBC].
d. perf. pass. participle of προλέγω (LN 33.281) (BAGD 1. p. 704): 'to be spoken beforehand', 'to be spoken before' [Alf, BNTC; KJV], 'to be spoken in advance' [Lns], 'to be foretold' [BAGD; NET], 'to be told ahead of time' [LN], 'to be told beforehand' [BAGD], 'to be told in the past' [TEV], 'to be proclaimed beforehand' [BAGD], 'to be predicted' [LN]. This passive verb is also translated as an active verb: 'to foretell' [AB; NIV, NJB]. It implies being spoken earlier [Alf, Hu, Law, TH, TNTC, WBC], as the prefixed preposition προ- implies [Hu, Law], not prophecy [Alf, Hu, TG]; it implies prophecy [Hie]; it implies both prior time and prophecy [Lg]. The perfect tense implies the continuing validity of the message [Hie, Law, Lns, NTC].
e. ὑπό with genitive object (LN 90.1): 'by' [Alf, BNTC, LN, Lns; CEV, NET, TEV], 'made by' [REB], 'of' [KJV], not explicit [NIV, NJB, NLT]. It indicates personal agent [Law].

QUESTION—What is the function of this verse?

It begins a contrast with the preceding [AB, BNTC, EBC, Hie, Hu, Lns], moving from describing the false teachers to addressing the believers [NTC, WBC]. This contrast is emphasized by ὑμεῖς δέ 'but you' [BNTC, Hu, Lns,

TH], by δὲ, ἀγαπητοί 'but, beloved' [NIBC], by all three introductory words ὑμεῖς δὲ, ἀγαπητοί 'but you, beloved' [Hie].

QUESTION—What relationship is indicated by ὑμεῖς 'you'?

It is an emphatic word [El, Law] and emphatic by forefronting [ICC, Law]; it contrasts with the οὗτοι 'these persons' in verse 16 [BNTC, ICC, Law, Lns].

QUESTION—To whom does τῶν ἀποστόλων τοῦ κυρίου Ἰησοῦ Χριστοῦ 'the apostles of our Lord Jesus Christ' refer?

It refers to the original Twelve [BNTC, TG, TH] plus Paul [EBC, Hie, NTC], specifically Peter and Paul [NTC]; it does not include the author [BNTC, Hie, Hu, ICC, Lg, NTC, TH, TNTC]. It refers to the apostles who founded the churches being addressed here [TNTC, WBC]. The phrase 'of our Lord Jesus Christ' indicates that they were Christ's representatives [Hie]; 'our' includes the author as committed to Jesus along with his readers [Hie, TH].

18 that they-were-saying to-you that at[a] (the) last[b] (of-the) time[c] there-will-be mockers[d]

TEXT—Some manuscripts omit ὅτι 'that' following ὑμῖν 'you'. GNT brackets this word, indicating doubt, but does not deal with it. The fact that ὅτι can be either left untranslated as introducing a direct quote or translated 'that' makes it impossible to determine whether some commentaries and English versions which translate the following words as a direct quotation include this word. This word is clearly included by Alf, El, Hie, ICC, CEV.

TEXT—Some manuscripts omit τοῦ 'the' before χρόνου 'time'. GNT brackets this word, indicating doubt, but does not deal with it. Since this word may be read without specifically translating it, it is difficult to tell whether this word is read unless it is specifically referred to or noted in the Greek text. It is included by Law, NIBC, WBC; it is included in brackets by Alf; it is omitted by ICC, Lg.

LEXICON—a. ἐπί with genitive object (LN 67.33) (BAGD I.2. p. 286): 'at' [AB, Alf, LN, Lns; NJB], 'in' [BAGD, BNTC, WBC; all versions except CEV, NJB, TEV], 'near' [CEV], 'when come' [TEV].
b. ἔσχατος (LN 61.13) (BAGD 3.b. p. 314): 'last' [Alf, BAGD, BNTC, LN; all versions except CEV, NET, NJB, REB], 'end' [Lns; CEV, NET], 'final' [AB, WBC; REB], 'final point' [NJB].
c. χρόνος (LN 67.78) (BAGD p. 888): 'time' [AB, Alf, BAGD, BNTC, LN, Lns; CEV, KJV, NET, NJB, NRSV, TNT], 'age' [WBC; REB]; this singular noun is translated as a plural: 'times' [ISV, NIV, NLT], 'days' [NAB, TEV].
d. ἐμπαίκτης (LN **33.407**) (BAGD p. 255): 'mocker' [BAGD, LN, Lns; KJV, NJB], 'scoffer' [AB, Alf, BNTC, WBC; NET, NIV, NLT, NRSV], 'skeptic' [ISV], 'impostor' [NAB], 'one who mocks at religion' [REB]. This noun is also translated as a verb: 'to mock' [TNT], 'to make fun of' [TEV]. It means despisers of morality and religion [BNTC, Hie, WBC], persons who make fun of holy things [Alf, Hu, NTC], who make fun of

God, the gospel, and Christians who live by the gospel [TH], who deride teachings about the return of Christ and the resurrection [Blm], who laugh at those who refuse to join them in their impious desires [TNTC].

QUESTION—What kind of quotation is this?
1. It is translated as a direct quotation [AB, BNTC, Hie, ICC, Lns, WBC; all versions except CEV, KJV, NLT]: they were saying, "At the last . . . impieties."
2. It is translated as an indirect quotation [Alf, El, Lg(M); CEV, KJV, NLT]: they were saying that at the last . . . impieties.

QUESTION—What is implied by the phrase ἔλεγον ὑμῖν 'they were saying to you'?

It means that the apostles' message was intended for Christians of all times [BNTC, TH]. It refers to repeated warnings [Hie, Law, NTC] as the imperfect tense implies [Law, NTC, TBST, TNTC], indicating emphasis [Law]. It shows that the readers were familiar with the warnings [Hie, NIBC].
1. The quotation is intended as a summary of the predictions by the prophets and Christ's apostles, not a specific quotation [BNTC, CBC, Hu, TBST]. It indicates that the readers had heard the warnings from the apostles themselves [Hu, NTC]. It is not a reference to 2 Peter [NIBC].
2. It is a quotation from 2 Peter [Lg].

QUESTION—To what does the phrase ἐπ' ἐσχάτου τοῦ χρόνου 'at the last of the time' refer?
1. It refers to the last of the present age [Law], the end of the world [Alf, Hu], the day of salvation and of judgment [BNTC, EBC] and the return of Christ [EBC, NIBC].
2. It refers to the present age between Christ's earthly life and his second coming [Hie, NTC, TBST, TH].

QUESTION—How are the two nouns related in the genitive construction ἐσχάτου τοῦ χρόνου 'last of the time'?
1. The genitive noun χρόνου 'time' governs the adjective ἐσχάτου 'last' [Lns; NJB]; it is a partitive genitive: the last (part of) time.
2. The adjective ἐσχάτου 'last' describes the genitive noun χρόνου 'time' [AB, BNTC, Hie, WBC; all versions except CEV, NJB]: the last time. It states the character of the 'time' [Hie].

going[a] according-to[b] their-own desires[c] of the impieties.[d]

LEXICON—a. pres. mid. (deponent = act.) participle of πορεύω: 'to go'. See this word in verse 16. This entire phrase is translated 'selfish and godless people would start making fun of God' [CEV], 'whose purpose in life is to enjoy themselves in every evil way imaginable' [NLT]. The present tense indicates habitual practice [Law].

b. κατά with accusative object (LN 89.8): 'according to'. See this word in verse 16.

c. ἐπιθυμία (LN 25.12) (BAGD 3. p. 293): 'desire'. See this word in verse 16.

d. ἀσέβεια (LN 53.10) (BAGD p. 114): 'impiety' [Alf], 'godlessness' [LN], 'ungodliness' [Lns, WBC], not explicit [NLT]. This noun is also translated as an adjective: 'godless' [AB, BAGD; CEV, NAB, NJB, TEV], 'ungodly' [BNTC; KJV, NET, NIV, NRSV, REB]; as a verb phrase: 'to have no interest in religion' [TNT]. It is emphatic by its position [EGT, Hie, Hu, NTC], to emphasize the character of the false teachers [Hu, Lg, NTC]. This word is redundant here [ICC].

QUESTION—What relationship is indicated by the participle πορευόμενοι 'going'?
  1. It is attributive [AB, WBC; KJV, NIV, NJB, NLT, REB, TEV, TNT]: mockers, who go.
  2. It is a predicate relationship: mockers, (and they are) going.

QUESTION—How are the two nouns related in the genitive construction ἐπιθυμίας τῶν ἀσεβειῶν 'desires of the impieties'?
  1. The genitive noun ἀσεβειῶν 'of impieties' describes ἐπιθυμίας 'desires' [AB, BAGD, Blm, BNTC(text), TH; all versions except CEV, NLT, TNT]: impious desires.
  2. The genitive noun ἀσεβειῶν 'of impieties' states the source of the desires [EGT, Law]: desires arising from impieties.
  3. The genitive noun ἀσεβειῶν 'of impieties' states the goal of the ἐπιθυμίας 'desires' [BNTC(comment), Hie, Lns, WBC] as an objective genitive [Lns]: the desires for impieties.

19 These (persons) are the-(ones) causing-divisions/separating,ᵃ

TEXT—Some manuscripts add ἑαυτούς 'themselves' after ἀποδιορίζοντες 'causing-divisions/separating'. GNT omits this word with an A decision, indicating that the text is certain. Only KJV includes this word.

LEXICON—a. pres. act. participle of ἀποδιορίζω (LN **30.116**, **39.16**) (BAGD p. 90): 'to cause divisions' [LN (**39.16**); ISV, NAB, NRSV, TEV, TNT], 'to cause division' [NJB], 'to cause a division' [BAGD], 'to create division' [AB], 'to create divisions' [WBC; NLT, REB], 'to set up divisions' [BNTC], 'to make divisions' [Lns], 'to divide' [NIV], 'to be divisive' [NET], 'to draw a line between' [LN (**30.116**)], 'to make a distinction between' [LN (30.116)], 'to separate' [Alf; KJV], 'to separate one from another' [LN (30.116)], 'to make (persons) turn against (each other)' [CEV].

QUESTION—What relationship is indicated by οὗτοι 'these'?
  It is a contemptuous reference, as in verses 12 and 16 [NIBC, TNTC].

QUESTION—What is meant by ἀποδιορίζοντες 'making-divisions/causing-divisions/ separating'?
  The use of this participle without an object places emphasis on the activity itself [Hie]. The present tense implies continuing action [Law, Lg(M), TBST].

1. It means to cause divisions [AB, Blm, BNTC, Lns, NTC, WBC; all versions except CEV, KJV, NIV], to cause separations [El, Hie, ICC, Law], to make invidious distinctions [EGT], to divide the believers from one another [Hie, Lns, NTC; NIV]. They were not outwardly separating themselves from the church [Hie, Law, Lg, TH], but their teaching was causing divisions within the church [Hie, Law, NTC, TBST, TH]; they were separating themselves by wealth, class, and assuming intellectual superiority [ICC]. They were making themselves an exclusive circle [NIBC, TNTC, WBC]; they were making a distinction between spiritual and unspiritual persons [CBC, EBC, LN (30.116), TBST].
2. It refers to turning people against each other [CEV].
3. It means that these persons are separating from others in the church, drawing their own lines of distinction between themselves and the congregation [Alf, TG]. They assumed that they were superior Christians and separated from the others by their attitudes and way of life [TG].
4. With the addition of ἑαυτούς 'themselves', it means that these persons separate themselves from others [KJV].

soulish,ᵃ not having (the) Spirit/spirit.ᵇ

LEXICON—a. ψυχικός (LN 41.41, 79.2) (BAGD 2.b. p. 894): 'soulish', 'unspiritual' [LN (41.41)], 'worldly' [BAGD, LN (41.41); ISV, NET, REB], 'worldly-minded' [BNTC; TNT], 'worldly people' [NRSV], 'sensual' [Alf; KJV], 'natural' [LN (41.41, 79.2)], 'physical' [AB, LN (79.2), Lns]. This adjective is also translated as a noun: 'sensualist' [NAB]; as a clause: 'they think only about this life' [CEV], 'who live according to nature' [NJB], 'who follow mere natural instincts' [WBC; NIV], 'who are controlled by their natural desires' [TEV], 'they live by natural instinct' [NLT]. This word means the opposite of 'spiritual' [AB, ICC, Lns], implying not having God's Spirit [AB, BNTC, TNTC]; it means to think only of one's self and one's own interests [Alf], to live on the level of natural instincts [BNTC, EBC, Hie, Lg, Lns, TBST, TH, TNTC, WBC], to be ruled by human reasoning and emotions [El].
b. πνεῦμα (LN 12.18) (BAGD 5.d.β. p. 677): 'Spirit' [AB, BAGD, BNTC, LN, WBC; ISV, KJV, NAB, NET, NIV, NJB, NRSV, TEV], 'Holy Spirit' [LN], 'God's Spirit' [CEV, NLT], 'Spirit of God' [LN], 'spirit' [Alf, Lns]. The phrase πνεῦμα μὴ ἔχοντες 'not having the Spirit/spirit' is translated 'unspiritual' [REB, TNT]. This word is emphatic by forefronting [Law].

QUESTION—What is implied by the phrase πνεῦμα μὴ ἔχοντες 'not having the Spirit/spirit'?

This phrase explains ψυχικοί 'soulish' [TG, WBC]. It means unconverted [Lns, NIBC, TBST], unbelieving, without God, dead in sin [Law].

QUESTION—What is meant by πνεῦμα 'Spirit/spirit'?

1. It refers to the Holy Spirit [AB, BNTC, EBC, EGT, Hie, Hu, Law, TBST, TH, WBC; CEV, NAB, NET, NJB, NLT, NRSV, TEV].

JUDE 1:19   69

    2. It refers to the human inner life [Alf, ICC; REB, TNT], to the rational spirit [Lg], to spiritual insight and power [El].

QUESTION—What relationship is indicated by the participle ἔχοντες 'having'? The present tense implies a continuing state [Law].
    1. It is attributive [BAGD, LN (30.116); NIV, NJB, TEV]: who do not have the Spirit.
    2. It is causal [El; NLT].
    2.1 Because they do not have the Spirit [NLT].
    2.2 Because they do not have spiritual insight and power [El].
    3. It is translated as a separate proposition [AB; CEV]: they don't have the Spirit.

DISCOURSE UNIT: 20–25 [Law]. The topic is believers' responsibility during times of apostasy.

DISCOURSE UNIT: 20–23 [EGT, TNTC, WBC; NAB, NJB]. The topic is the appeal [WBC], Christian admonitions [NAB], the duties of love [NJB], the final exhortation to the faithful ones [EGT, TNTC].

DISCOURSE UNIT: 20–21 [Hie, TBST]. The topic is directions for security amid apostasy [Hie], the faithful Christian contending for the faith [TBST].

20 **But you, beloved,ª building-upᵇ yourselves in-your most-holyᶜ faith,**

LEXICON—a. ἀγαπητός (LN 25.45) (BAGD 2. p. 6): 'beloved' [AB, Alf, LN, Lns; KJV, NAB, NRSV], 'one who is loved' [LN], 'friend' [REB, TEV, TNT], 'dear friend' [BAGD, BNTC, WBC; CEV, ISV, NET, NIV, NJB, NLT], 'dear' [LN]. It calls attention back to the believers [EBC] and contrasts them with the false teachers [NTC, TNTC]. It means loved by God [NIBC, NTC].
    b. pres. act. participle of ἐποικοδομέω (LN **74.15**) (BAGD 2. p. 305): 'to build (oneself) up' [AB, Alf, BNTC, **LN**, Lns, WBC; ISV, KJV, NET, NIV, NJB, NRSV, TEV, TNT], 'to build each other up' [BAGD], 'to build up' [LN], 'to build (one's) life' [NLT], 'to build on (a) foundation' [CEV], 'to grow strong' [NAB], 'to strengthen, to make more able' [LN]. The phrase ἐποικοδομοῦντες ἑαυτοὺς τῇ ἁγιωτάτῃ ὑμῶν πίστει 'building up yourselves in your most holy faith' is translated 'you must make your most sacred faith the foundation of your lives' [REB]. The present tense refers to continuing action [EBC, Hie, Law, TBST; CEV, NLT, TEV]. It refers to developing inner maturity [Hie], spiritual growth [NIBC], Christian knowledge and grace [Law].
    c. ἁγιώτατος (LN 88.24) (BAGD 1.a.α. p. 9): 'most holy' [Alf, BAGD, BNTC, LN, Lns, WBC; CEV, ISV, KJV, NET, NIV, NJB, NRSV, TNT], 'most sacred' [AB; REB, TEV], 'holy' [NAB, NLT]. It is here a true superlative, 'most holy' [Hie, Law, Lns, NTC]; it is intensive, 'very holy' [ICC, TH]. It implies a faith revealed by a holy God [BNTC, EGT, Hie, NIBC, NTC, TBST, WBC] and that was intended to make people holy [Blm, BNTC, EGT, Hie, NIBC, TBST, TNTC]. It is 'most holy' because

it concerns Jesus, God's holy servant [EBC]. It is in contrast with the most unholy teachings of the false teachers [El, Hie, Lg]. It is utterly unique and different from all other faiths [TNTC].

QUESTION—What is implied by the introductory phrase, ὑμεῖς δέ, ἀγαπητοί 'but you, beloved'?

It implies a strong contrast between the readers and the false teachers [BNTC, EGT, Hie, Hu]. Ὑμεῖς 'you' is in emphatic contrast with the false teachers [El]; δέ 'but' establishes the contrast [Law].

QUESTION—What relationship is indicated by the present participle ἐποικοδομοῦντες 'building up'?

1. It has imperative meaning [AB, Hu, TNTC, WBC; all versions except KJV, NET] governed by the imperative τηρήσατε 'keep' in verse 21 [Hie, Hu]: build yourselves up. It indicates one of the means for the exhortation in verse 21 [Hie, Hu]; it is a more precise statement of the means, whereas the following προσευχόμενοι 'praying' is more general [Hu].
2. It is translated as means [Lns; NET]: by building yourselves up.

QUESTION—What relationship is indicated by ἑαυτούς 'yourselves'?

1. It means 'yourselves', not 'one another' [Alf, Hie, Hu, ICC, Law, Lg].
2. The plural implies the reciprocal sense, building up one another [TBST, WBC].

QUESTION—What relationship is indicated by the dative phrase τῇ ἁγιωτάτῃ πίστει 'the most holy faith'?

1. It indicates the foundation for 'building up' [Alf, Hie, Hu, Law, TH, WBC; CEV, NJB, NLT]: building yourselves up on the foundation which is the most holy faith.
2. It indicates the means for 'building up' [AB, Lns]: by means of the most holy faith/faithfulness.

QUESTION—What relationship is indicated by πίστει 'faith'?

1. 'Faith' refers to the things which are believed [Alf], faith in Christ [Law], the gospel [WBC]; it refers to the sum of apostolic teaching [BNTC, EBC, Hie, Hu, ICC, Lg, Lns, TBST, TH, TNTC]; it deals with the holy character and redemptive work of Christ [Hie].
2. It refers to being faithful [AB].

praying in[a] (the) Holy Spirit,

LEXICON—a. ἐν with dative object (LN 13.8, 89.119, 90.6): 'in' [AB, Alf, BNTC, LN (13.8, 89.119), WBC; ISV, KJV, NAB, NET, NIV, NJB, NRSV], 'in union with' [LN (89.119)], 'in connection with' [Lns], 'in the power of' [REB, TEV, TNT], 'by' [LN (90.6)], 'as . . . helps' [CEV], 'as you are directed by' [NLT]. The meaning is 'on the basis of' [BAGD under ἐποικοδομέω 'to build up'], 'in the control of' [TH].

QUESTION—What relationship is indicated by the participle προσευχόμενοι 'praying'?

The present tense indicates continuing action [EBC, Hie, Law, TBST; NLT, REB].

1. It has imperative meaning [Hu, TNTC, WBC; ISV, NIV, NLT, NRSV, REB, TEV, TNT] governed by the imperative τηρήσατε 'keep' in verse 21 [Hie, Hu]: pray. It indicates one of the means for the exhortation in verse 21 [Hie, Hu].
2. It is translated as temporal [Lns]: while you pray.
3. It indicates means [Alf; NAB]: by means of praying.

QUESTION—What relationship is indicated by the preposition ἐν 'in'?

The prepositional phrase ἐν πνεύματι ἁγίῳ 'in the Holy Spirit' is emphatic by forefronting [Law]. It includes (may include [TNTC]) praying in tongues [NIBC, WBC] but also simply to pray [TNTC, WBC]; it means merely to pray [TBST].
1. It expresses agency [Blm; NLT] and influence [Blm], controlled by [WBC], the means, the source of the power [El, Hu; REB, TEV, TNT]: in the power of the Holy Spirit, as the Holy Spirit directs.
2. It indicates the sphere of action, implying being immersed in the Spirit [Hie, Law].
3. It expresses a connection with the preceding word πίστει 'faith' [Lns]: your most holy faith in connection with the Holy Spirit.

21 keep[a] yourselves in[b] (the) love of-God,

LEXICON—a. aorist act. impera. of τηρέω (LN 13.32) (BAGD 2.b. p. 815): 'to keep' [AB, Alf, BAGD, BNTC, LN, Lns, WBC; KJV, NIV, NJB, NRSV, REB, TEV, TNT], 'to remain' [ISV], 'to persevere' [NAB], 'to maintain' [NET], 'to keep in step' [CEV]. This entire clause is translated 'live in such a way that God's love can bless you' [NLT]. It implies keeping oneself from harm [BAGD]. The aorist tense refers to one life-long act [Alf]; the aorist imperative implies urgency [EGT].
b. ἐν with dative object (LN 83.13): 'in' [AB, Alf, BNTC, LN, Lns, WBC; all versions except CEV, NJB, NLT], 'within' [NJB], 'with' [CEV].

QUESTION—What relationship is indicated by ἑαυτούς 'yourselves'?

This word is emphatic by forefronting [Hie, Law].
1. It is reflexive, implying 'each one keeping himself' [EGT, Hie, ICC, Law, Lns].
2. It has the reciprocal sense [Blm]: keep each other.

QUESTION—How are the two nouns related in the genitive construction ἀγάπῃ θεοῦ 'love of God'?
1. The genitive noun θεοῦ 'God' tells who it is who loves [Alf, BNTC, EBC, El, Hie, Hu, ICC, Law, Lg, Lns, NIBC, NTC, TH, TNTC, WBC]: God's love for you. They keep themselves in God's love by showing that his love so controls them that they want to please him [TG]. It means that they are to live so that God can give them all the gifts that he gives to those he loves [Lns]. They must respond to God's love [NIBC]. They must avoid backsliding which would cause them to lose their awareness of his love and they do this by keeping his commandments [BNTC]. They

receive his love when they strive to do God's will and obey him [ICC, NTC].
2. The genitive noun θεοῦ 'God' tells who is loved [Blm]: your love for God.

awaiting[a] the mercy[b] of our Lord Jesus Christ for[c] life eternal.
LEXICON—a. pres. mid. (deponent = act.) participle of προσδέχομαι (LN 34.53, 85.60) (BAGD 2.b. p. 712): 'to await' [AB], 'to wait for' [LN (85.60), WBC; CEV, NIV, NJB, NLT, TEV, TNT], 'to look for' [Alf; ISV, KJV], 'to look forward to' [BNTC; NRSV, REB], 'to expect' [Lns], 'to anticipate' [NET], 'to welcome' [LN (34.53); NAB]. The present tense implies a habitual state [Alf, Law]; it implies eagerly expecting [Hie, Law].
b. ἔλεος (LN 88.76) (BAGD 3. p. 250): 'mercy' [AB, Alf, BNTC, LN, Lns, WBC; all versions except CEV]. The phrase τὸ ἔλεος τοῦ κυρίου ἡμῶν Ἰησοῦ Χριστοῦ 'the mercy of our Lord Jesus Christ' is translated 'our Lord Jesus Christ to show how kind he is' [CEV]. It refers to the mercy which Christ will show to his people at his return [Alf, Hu, Law, Lg, Lns, TH, WBC], the mercy given in Christ's atoning death [TNTC].
c. εἰς with accusative object (LN 78.51, 89.57, 90.23): 'for' [Lns], 'for the purpose of' [LN (89.57)], 'to the point of' [LN (88.76)], 'unto' [AB, Alf, BNTC; KJV], 'concerning' [LN (90.23)], 'that brings' [ISV, NET], 'that leads to' [NRSV], 'to bring you to' [NIV], 'to give you' [NJB], 'to grant you' [WBC], 'which leads to' [NAB], 'by giving you' [CEV]. It indicates 'bringing (you) to' [Blm, EBC].
QUESTION—What relationship is indicated by the participle προσδεχόμενοι 'awaiting'?
1. It is temporal [NTC; CEV, ISV, NIV, NLT, TEV]: while you await.
2. It is translated as an imperative [AB, WBC; NAB, NJB, NRSV, REB]: and welcome.
QUESTION—How are the two nouns related in the genitive construction τὸ ἔλεος τοῦ κυρίου... 'the mercy of the Lord ...'?
The genitive noun κυρίου 'Lord' states who shows the mercy [Alf, Hie].
QUESTION—What relationship is indicated by the full phrase τοῦ κυρίου ἡμῶν Ἰησοῦ Χριστοῦ 'our Lord Jesus Christ'?
It unites the author with his readers in the expressed hope [Hie].
QUESTION—What is the phrase εἰς ζωὴν αἰώνιον 'for life eternal' connected with?
1. It is connected with τὸ ἔλεος 'the mercy' [BNTC, EGT; ISV, NAB, NET, NIV, NJB, NRSV]: the mercy which brings life eternal.
2. It is connected with τηρήσατε 'keep' [El, Hu, ICC, Law, Lg]: keep yourselves for life eternal.
3. It is connected with προσδεχόμενοι τὸ ἔλεος 'awaiting the mercy' [Hie, Lg(M), Lns]: awaiting the mercy for life eternal.

DISCOURSE UNIT: 22–23 [Hie]. The topic is duty toward victims of apostasy.

22 And some on-the-one-hand have-mercy-on[a] doubting[b1]/making-a-distinction,[b2]

TEXT—Instead of ἐλεᾶτε 'have mercy on', some manuscripts read ἐλέγχετε 'reprove'. Instead of the accusative plural participle διακρινομένους 'doubting' (referring to the persons being dealt with), some manuscripts read the nominative plural διακρινόμενοι (referring to the subject of the verb). One very ancient manuscript transposes this clause with the following clause (see also at v. 23) and reads this verse (v. 22) as οὓς μὲν ἐκ πυρὸς ἁρπάσατε 'some on the one hand snatch from (the) fire'. GNT reads ἐλεᾶτε 'have mercy on', the accusative plural participle, and does not accept the transposition, with a C decision, indicating that the Committee had difficulty in making the decision. Ἐλέγχετε 'reprove' is read by Alf, EGT, El, Hu, Lg, Lns, TNTC, NAB; the nominative plural participle διακρινόμενοι is read by Blm and KJV; the transposition of clauses (see also at v. 23) is read by AB, ICC (with some variation), and WBC.

LEXICON—a. pres. act. impera. of ἐλεάω (LN 88.76) (BAGD p. 249): 'to have mercy on' [AB, BAGD, LN, WBC; NET, NRSV], 'to show mercy' [LN], 'to show mercy to' [ISV, NLT], 'to show mercy toward' [TEV], 'to be merciful toward' [LN], 'to be merciful to' [NIV], 'to have compassion' [KJV], 'to be compassionate to' [NJB], 'to have pity' [BNTC], 'to show pity' [TNT], 'to be helpful to' [CEV]. This entire clause is translated 'there are some doubting souls who need your pity' [REB]; different text: 'to correct' [NAB], 'to convict' [Alf], 'to rebuke' [Lns]. The present tense (of either verb) implies an attitude whenever the need arises [Hie, Lns].

b. (b[1]) accusative plural pres. mid. (deponent = act.) participle of διακρίνομαι (LN 31.37) (BAGD 2.b. p. 185): 'to doubt' [BAGD, LN; NIV, REB], 'to have doubts' [CEV, ISV, TEV], 'to be in doubt' [TNT], 'to be confused' [NAB], 'to waver' [BAGD; NET, NJB, NRSV], 'to hesitate' [BNTC], 'to dispute' [AB, Lns, WBC], 'to contend' [Alf]. This participle is translated as a clause: 'whose faith is wavering' [NLT]. It means to dispute [EGT, Lg], to doubt [El, Hie, Law, Lg(M), NIBC, TBST, TH].

b. (b[2]) nominative plural pres. mid. participle of διακρίνω (LN 30.113): 'to make a distinction' [LN], 'to make a difference' [KJV].

QUESTION—To whom does this clause refer?

1. Reading ἐλεᾶτε 'have mercy on', it refers to those who have not gone very far astray [BNTC, CBC, El, Hie, Law, NIBC, NTC, TBST, TG, TH] and who can be dealt with compassionately [Blm, EBC, Hie, NTC, TBST]. Their doubts are about the Christian faith [TG].
2. Reading ἐλέγχετε 'reprove'.
2.1 This clause refers to those who must be convicted by argument [Alf, Lg, Lns, TNTC].

2.2 It refers to those who are to be punished and left to themselves [Hu].

QUESTION—What relationship is indicated by οὓς μέν 'some on the one hand'?

It distinguishes the persons described here from those in the following clause [Hie, Lg(M)].

QUESTION—What relationship is indicated by the participle διακρινομένους 'making a distinction'?

    1. It refers to οὕς 'some', the recipients of the mercy.
      1.1 It is attributive [AB, BNTC, Law, Lns, WBC; all versions except KJV, NJB]: have mercy on some who have doubts.
      1.2 It is causal [NJB]: have mercy on some because they have doubts.
      1.3 It is temporal [Alf]: have mercy on some when they contend.
    2. For those who read the nominative plural διακρινόμενοι 'making a difference', it refers to those who are to show mercy [KJV].

23 on-the-other-hand save^a some snatching^b from^c (the) fire,^d

TEXT—(See also at v. 22.) Some manuscripts add ἐν φόβῳ 'in fear' before σῴζετε 'save' or at the end of this clause. One very ancient manuscript transposes this clause with the preceding clause and reads the present clause as διακρινομένους δὲ ἐλεεῖτε ἐν φόβῳ 'and doubting (ones) have mercy on with fear'. GNT rejects both of these changes with a C decision, indicating that the Committee had difficulty in deciding the text. Ἐν φόβῳ 'in fear' is added by AB, Blm, Lg, and KJV. The modified transposition is read by AB, ICC (with some variation), and WBC.

LEXICON—a. pres. act. impera. of σῴζω (LN 21.18, 21.27) (BAGD 2.a.β. p. 798): 'to save' [Alf, BAGD, BNTC, LN (21.27), Lns; all versions except CEV, NAB, NLT], 'to rescue' [LN (21.18); CEV, NAB, NLT], 'to deliver' [LN (21.18)]; different text: [AB, WBC]. The present tense implies attempting to save [Alf, El] whenever the need arises [Hie]; it implies continuing action [Law, Lns]. To save is God's work, but the meaning here is that he desires to use his people in the work of salvation [Hie, Law, NTC].

b. pres. act. participle of ἁρπάζω (LN 18.4) (BAGD 2.a. p. 109): 'to snatch' [AB, Alf, BAGD, BNTC, Lns, WBC; all versions except CEV, KJV], 'to snatch away, to seize' [LN], 'to rescue' [CEV], 'to pull' [KJV]. This word implies aggressive action [Hie, Hu, Law, Lg].

c. ἐκ with genitive object (LN 84.4): 'from' [AB, Alf, BNTC, LN, WBC; all versions except KJV, NRSV, TEV], 'out from' [LN], 'out of' [LN, Lns; KJV, NET, NRSV, TEV].

d. πῦρ (LN 2.3) (BAGD 1.a. p. 730): 'fire' [AB, Alf, BAGD, BNTC, LN, Lns, WBC; all versions except NLT, REB]. This singular noun is translated as a plural: 'flames' [REB], 'flames of judgment' [NLT]. It refers to the fire of punishment in hell at the judgment day [BNTC, EBC, Hie, Lg, NIBC, TG]; it refers to the fire of their present danger [El, Hu], their

JUDE 1:23

present sin [NTC]; it refers primarily to the hell in this life resulting from their lives and teachings [Alf].

QUESTION—To whom does this clause refer?

It refers to the second group, those who are in greater spiritual danger than the preceding group [Hie, Hu, Lns, TBST, TNTC]. They have accepted the false teachings [TNTC].

QUESTION—What relationship is indicated by the participle ἁρπάζοντες 'snatching'?

1. It expresses means [BNTC, Lns; ISV, NET, NJB, NLT, NRSV, REB, TEV, TNT]: by means of snatching them.
2. It expresses manner [CEV]: as you would snatch them.
3. It is translated as an imperative [NIV]: snatch them.

QUESTION—What is the phrase ἐκ πυρός 'from the fire' connected with?

It is connected with ἁρπάζοντες 'snatching' [AB, BNTC, ICC, Lns, WBC; all versions]: snatching them from the fire.

and some have-mercy-on[a] in[b] fear,

TEXT—Some manuscripts omit this clause. GNT includes it with a C decision, indicating that the Committee had difficulty making the decision. This clause is omitted by AB, Blm, KJV.

LEXICON—a. pres. act. impera. of ἐλεάω: 'to have mercy on'. See this word in verse 22.

b. ἐν with dative object (LN 13.8, 89.80, 89.84): 'in' [Alf, LN (13.8), Lns], 'with' [AB, BNTC, LN (13.8, 89.80, 89.84), WBC; CEV, ISV, KJV, NRSV], 'mixed with' [NIV, REB, TEV], 'coupled with' [NET], 'mingled with' [TNT]. The phrase ἐν φόβῳ 'in fear' is translated 'be on your guard' [NAB], 'be wary' [NJB], 'but be careful' [NLT].

QUESTION—To whom does this clause refer?

1. It refers to the third class of persons [El, Hie, Hu, Law, Lns, NTC, TBST, TNTC]
   1.1 This group are those who can be rescued and who are to be brought back by saving help [Hu, TBST, TNTC], but with great caution [Hie].
   1.2 This group are those most degraded spiritually [El, Hie, Lns]; they are beyond help and can only be pitied [Lns].
   1.3 Reading ἐλέγχετε 'reprove' in verse 22 instead of ἐλεᾶτε 'have mercy on', this group are the least corrupted spiritually [Hu].
2. Following a different text, it refers to the second of two classes of persons [AB, WBC].

QUESTION—What relationship is indicated by the phrase ἐν φόβῳ 'in fear'?

1. It refers to fear of defilement by the false teachings and lives of the false teachers [Alf, CBC, EBC, El, Hie, Hu, ICC, Law, Lns, NIBC, NTC, TG, TH; NLT]; they are to use caution in dealing with these people [TH]. They must fear that they themselves would be influenced by the sins of those people, or that the believers in the church might be led to commit sin by those who are restored to fellowship [TG].

2. It refers to the fear of thinking too lightly of the sin involved [EGT].
3. It is the awesome religious fear of God [BNTC; NET], fear of God's judgment [TNTC, WBC].

QUESTION—What is the phrase ἐν φόβῳ 'in fear' connected with?
1. It is connected with ἐλεᾶτε 'have mercy on' [AB, Alf, BNTC, Lns, WBC; all versions except KJV]: have mercy with fear in your heart. It means that the rescuers must fear becoming involved in the corruption [Lg(M)].
2. Different text, placing this phrase to modify σῴζετε 'save' in the preceding clause [Lg; KJV]; it means to use the motive of fear in persuading them [Lg].

hating[a] even[b] the tunic[c] stained[d] from[e] the flesh.[f]

LEXICON—a. pres. act. participle of μισέω (LN 88.198) (BAGD 2. p. 523): 'to hate' [AB, Alf, BAGD, BNTC, LN, Lns, WBC; all versions except NAB, NLT], 'to detest' [BAGD, LN], 'abhor' [BAGD; NAB]. This entire phrase is translated 'that you aren't contaminated by their sins' [NLT]. It refers to a feeling of aversion against the moral pollution [Hie].
b. καί (LN 89.93) (BAGD II.2. p. 393): 'even' [AB, Alf, BAGD, LN, Lns, WBC; CEV, ISV, KJV, NET, NIV, NJB, NRSV], 'so much as' [NAB], '(the) very' [BNTC; REB, TEV, TNT]. This word adds emphasis to the thought [Hu, Lg].
c. χιτών (LN 6.162, 6.176) (BAGD p. 882): 'tunic' [BAGD, LN (6.176), Lns; NJB, NRSV], 'shirt' [BAGD, LN (6.176)], 'clothes' [LN (6.162); CEV, ISV, NET, TEV], 'clothing' [BNTC, WBC; NAB, NIV, REB], 'garment' [AB, Alf; KJV], 'garments' [TNT]. The reference is to literal garments [Alf, BNTC, EBC], the inner garment worn next to the body [BNTC, Hie, Hu, ICC, Law, Lns, NIBC, NTC, TH, TNTC, WBC] and soiled by the body [BNTC, WBC], by bodily discharges [NTC], by contact with the flesh made unclean by immorality [Hu, Lg(M)]; it is symbolic of anything which shares in the moral destruction by external contact [Hu]. It symbolizes whatever is associated with outward appearance and habits [Lg].
d. perf. pass. participle of σπιλόω (LN **79.58**) (BAGD p. 762): 'to be stained' [AB, BAGD, LN; ISV, NIV, NJB, TEV, TNT], 'to be spotted' [LN; KJV], 'to become spotted' [Lns], 'to be defiled' [BAGD; NRSV], 'to receive defilement' [Alf], 'to be contaminated' [BNTC; REB], 'to be soiled' [WBC; NET], 'to be made dirty' [CEV]. The phrase ἀπὸ τῆς σαρκὸς ἐσπιλωμένον 'stained from the flesh' is translated 'flesh-stained' [NAB] and represents iniquity [NTC]. The perfect tense implies a present state resulting from past corruption [Hie, Law, Lns].
e. ἀπό with genitive object (LN 90.11): 'from' [Alf, LN, Lns], 'by' [AB, BNTC, LN, WBC; all versions except NLT, REB], 'with' [REB].
f. σάρξ (LN 8.63) (BAGD 7. p. 744): 'flesh' [AB, Alf, BAGD, BNTC, LN, Lns, WBC; KJV, NAB, NET], 'corrupted flesh' [NIV], 'sensuality' [REB], 'sinful lust' [TNT]. This singular noun is translated as a plural:

'filthy deeds' [CEV], 'their sinful lives' [ISV], 'their sinful lusts' [TEV], 'their bodies' [NJB, NRSV]. It refers to the physical body [BNTC]; it refers to fallen human nature [Hie, TNTC; NET] as an active agency of evil [TNTC]. Here it refers to sins of the flesh committed by the false teachers [WBC].

QUESTION—What is the function of this phrase?

It explains the preceding phrase ἐν φόβῳ 'in fear' [Hu, TH]. It means that any physical contact with these persons is to be avoided, because of the corrupting influence of their immoral teachings and conduct [BNTC]. It is hyperbole, stating that these people are so sinful that even their clothes are defiled [TH, TNTC]. They are to avoid being contaminated by their sinful lives [TG]. They are to hate sin as they would hate filthy underclothes stained with excretions [NTC].

QUESTION—What relationship is indicated by the participle μισοῦντες 'hating'?

It is translated as an imperative [AB, Alf; CEV, NAB, REB, TEV, TNT]: hate even the tunic.

DISCOURSE UNIT: 24–25 [AB, BNTC, EBC, EGT, GNT, Hie, Lns, NTC, TBST, TG, TNTC, WBC; CEV, ISV, NAB, NIV, NJB, NLT, TEV]. The topic is the letter closing and doxology [AB], closing doxology [BNTC, Hie, Lns, TG, WBC], doxology [EBC, NTC, TNTC; NAB, NIV, NJB], benediction [GNT], final benediction and ascription [EGT], final prayer [CEV, ISV], a prayer of praise [NLT, TEV], contending for the faith: the salvation we share [TBST].

24 Now/But to-the-(one) being-able to-guard^a you not-stumbling^b

TEXT—Instead of ὑμᾶς 'you' some manuscripts read αὐτούς 'them' and other manuscripts read ἡμᾶς 'us'. Αὐτούς 'them' is read by Alf and possibly by El. 'Ημᾶς 'us' is not read by any.

LEXICON—a. aorist act. infin. of φυλάσσω (LN 37.120) (BAGD 1.c. p. 868): 'to guard' [AB, BAGD, Lns], 'to guard closely' [LN], 'to protect' [BAGD; NAB], 'to keep safe' [BNTC], 'to keep' [Alf, WBC; CEV, ISV, KJV, NET, NIV, NJB, NLT, NRSV, REB, TEV, TNT]. It means to guard [TNTC]; it implies protection against dangers [El, Hie, Lg, Lns, NTC, WBC]. The aorist tense implies effective guarding [Hie], the action in its entirety [NTC].

b. ἄπταιστος (LN **88.292**) (BAGD p. 102): 'not stumbling', 'non-stumbling' [Lns], 'without stumbling' [BAGD], 'from stumbling' [AB; NLT], 'free from stumbling' [LN, WBC], 'from falling' [CEV, ISV, KJV, NET, NIV, NJB, NRSV, REB, TEV, TNT], 'without falling' [Alf, BNTC], 'from a fall' [NAB], 'free from sinning' [**LN**]. The meaning is 'unfallen' [El], not offending [Hu], without stumbling [Hie, Lns], sure-footed [Hie], having moral and spiritual victory [Hie], not stumbling morally [ICC], not falling into error [Law]. It refers to being kept from ruin at the final judgment [BNTC].

JUDE 1:24

QUESTION—What is meant by δέ 'now/but'?

It closes off all other matters and introduces a summation [Alf, Hie], pointing out where all that is discussed in this epistle finds its ultimate solution [Hie, Lg(M)].

QUESTION—What relationship is implied by the participle τῷ δυναμένῳ 'the one being able'?

The verb used focuses on the ability of the one referred to rather than to his identity [Hie]; it refers to God [NTC, TG, TH]. The attributive present tense participle implies the ability as a continuing characteristic quality [Hie, Law], emphasizing God's power and sufficiency [TH].

QUESTION—What relationship is indicated by ὑμᾶς 'you'?

1. It applies the assurance of protection directly to the readers [Hie].
2. For those who read αὐτούς 'them' instead of ὑμᾶς 'you', it indicates that the author is speaking in the third person of his readers, as if he were praying to God for them [Alf, El].

and to-set[a] (you) in-the-presence-of[b] his glory[c] blameless[d] in[e] exultation,[f]

LEXICON—a. aorist act. infin. of ἵστημι (LN 85.40) (BAGD I.1.a. p. 382): 'to set' [Alf, BAGD, LN; REB], 'to place' [BAGD, LN, Lns], 'to put' [LN], 'to bring' [BAGD; NLT, TEV], 'to bring safe' [NJB], 'to present' [BNTC, WBC; KJV, NIV, TNT], 'to make' [CEV], 'to make stand' [AB, LN; NAB, NRSV], 'to cause to stand' [NET], 'to make to stand' [ISV]. The meaning is 'to make you stand', referring to the final judgment day [Hie, ICC, TG]; it means to put in front of [TH].

b. κατενώπιον (LN **83.33**) (BAGD a. p. 421): 'in the presence of' [BAGD, Lns, WBC; NAB, NRSV, REB], 'before the presence of' [Alf, BNTC; KJV], 'before' [AB, LN]. The phrase κατενώπιον τῆς δόξης αὐτοῦ 'in the presence of his glory' is translated 'before his glorious presence' [NET, NIV, TEV], 'in his glorious presence' [CEV, ISV, TNT], 'into his glorious presence' [NLT], 'to his glorious presence' [NJB]. This phrase implies 'in God's presence' [BNTC]. This word implies 'in the immediate presence of' [Hie, Law].

c. δόξα (LN 76.13, 79.18, 87.23) (BAGD 1.a. p. 203): 'glory' [AB, Alf, BAGD, BNTC, LN (79.18, 87.23), Lns, WBC; KJV, NAB, NRSV, REB], 'glorious power' [LN (76.13)], 'greatness' [LN (87.23)], 'splendor' [LN (79.18)], 'sublimity, majesty' [BAGD]. This noun is also translated as an adjective modifying 'presence': [CEV, ISV, NET, NIV, NJB, NLT, TEV, TNT]. It refers to God's presence [TH], God himself [WBC], his radiance and majesty [BNTC, Hie, TG, TH]. It refers to the glory which will be revealed at Christ's return [Alf, EGT, El, Lns], God's glory at the judgment day [Hu, TBST].

d. ἄμωμος (LN 79.61, 88.34) (BAGD 2.a. p. 48): 'blameless' [Alf, BAGD, LN (88.34); TNT], 'faultless' [BNTC, LN (88.34); KJV, TEV], 'without fault' [LN (88.34); NIV], 'without a fault' [ISV], 'without defect' [LN (79.61)], 'without blemish' [AB, LN (79.61), WBC; NET, NRSV], 'unblemished' [NAB], 'blemishless' [Lns], 'above reproach' [REB], 'innocent' [NJB], 'innocent of sin' [NLT], 'pure' [CEV], 'perfect' [LN (88.34)]. It implies moral purity [BNTC, TH], without sin's stains [Lg], without blame [Law, TNTC].

e. ἐν with dative object (LN 89.80): 'in' [Alf, Lns], 'with' [BNTC, LN, WBC; ISV, KJV, NRSV], 'and with' [NIV], 'while at the same time' [LN], 'and in' [AB], not explicit [NET]. This word introduces the environment in which the readers will be found [Alf, Hie].

f. ἀγαλλίασις (LN 25.132) (BAGD p.3): 'exultation' [BNTC, Lns], 'rejoicing' [WBC; ISV, NET, NRSV], 'great rejoicing' [Alf], 'joy' [AB], 'exceeding joy' [KJV], 'great joy' [NIV], 'great gladness, extreme gladness' [LN]. The phrase ἐν ἀγαλλιάσει 'with exultation' is translated 'full of exultation' [BAGD], 'full of joy' [BAGD], 'and joyful' [CEV, NJB, TEV], 'and with great joy' [NLT], 'and rejoicing' [TNT], 'and exultant' [NAB], 'jubilant' [REB]. It refers to believers' exuberance of triumphant joy [Alf, BNTC, Hie, TG] for their completed salvation [EBC, Hie, TG], for being 'blameless' [Law], when God reveals himself at the final day [BNTC, Hie]; it implies access to God's presence by his people [AB]. The dative case indicates manner [NTC]. This preposition goes with 'to set you in the presence of' [NET].

QUESTION—What relationship is indicated by καί 'and'?

It connects the following infinitive phrase to the preceding phrase as a further result (as the ultimate result [Hu]) of God's dealings with his people [Hie, Hu]. The first phrase states a negative, 'keep from . . . ' while the latter phrase states a positive, 'to present . . . ' [TBST].

25 **to-(the)-only[a] God our Savior[b] through[c] Jesus Christ our Lord (be/belong) glory,[d] majesty,[e] power,[f] and authority[g]**

TEXT—Some manuscripts add σοφῷ 'wise' following μόνῳ 'only'. GNT rejects this addition with an A decision, indicating that the text is certain. Σοφῷ 'wise' is added by KJV and in brackets by Blm.

TEXT—Some manuscripts omit διὰ Ἰησοῦ Χριστοῦ τοῦ κυρίου ἡμῶν 'through Jesus Christ our Lord'. GNT does not deal with this variant. This phrase is omitted by Blm and KJV.

TEXT—Some manuscripts insert καί 'and' following δόξα 'glory'. GNT does not deal with this variant. Καί 'and' is added by Blm and KJV; it is included by REB but probably for style and not by accepting the textual addition.

TEXT—Some manuscripts omit πρὸ παντὸς τοῦ αἰῶνος 'before all the age'. GNT does not deal with this variant. This phrase is omitted by Blm and KJV.

LEXICON—a. μόνος (LN 58.50) (BAGD 1.a.δ. p. 527): 'only' [AB, Alf, BAGD, BNTC, Lns, WBC; all versions except CEV, NLT], 'only one, alone' [LN], 'to him who alone is' [NLT], not explicit [CEV]. It is emphatic, contrasting with the false teachings about God [BNTC, EBC, TBST], contrasting with the polytheism of the Gentiles [ICC, Law]; it

implies that God is the only true God [EBC, ICC, NTC, TBST, TNTC, WBC].
b. σωτήρ (LN 21.31) (BAGD 1. p. 801): 'Savior' [Alf, BNTC, LN, Lns, WBC; all versions except NAB], 'savior' [BAGD; NAB]. The phrase σωτῆρι ἡμῶν 'our Savior' is translated 'who saves us' [AB]. It refers to God the Father [AB, Alf, Blm, BNTC, EBC, Hu, ICC, Law, Lg, NIBC, NTC, TH, TNTC, WBC; NLT].
c. διά with genitive object (LN 90.4): 'through' [AB, Alf, BNTC, LN, Lns, WBC; all versions except CEV; different text: KJV], 'by' [LN], 'because of' [CEV].
d. δόξα (LN 87.4): 'glory' [AB, Alf, BNTC, Lns, WBC; all versions], 'honor, respect' [LN]. This word implies splendor and light [NIBC, TNTC], the radiance (and moral splendor [EBC]) which is inherent in God's nature and activity [BNTC, Hie, Law, Lns, NTC, WBC], the public presence of God [TBST].
e. μεγαλωσύνη (LN **87.21**) (BAGD p. 497): 'majesty' [AB, Alf, BAGD, BNTC, Lns, WBC; all versions except CEV], 'prominence' [**LN**], 'greatness' [BAGD, LN], 'importance' [LN], 'honor' [CEV]. It implies kingly majesty [TNTC]; it refers to God as king and absolute ruler [Lns], to God's greatness [EBC, Hie, Law] and power [Hie], to his awesome transcendence [BNTC, TBST, WBC], to his awesome splendor [TH], to his eternal right to rule [TBST], which makes him honored above all [Law].
f. κράτος (LN 76.6) (BAGD 4. p. 449): 'power' [BAGD, LN, WBC; all versions except KJV, NAB, TEV], 'might' [AB, Alf, LN, Lns; NAB, TEV], 'sovereignty, rule' [BAGD], 'dominion' [BNTC; KJV]. It refers to God's absolute power [BNTC, Hie, Law, Lg, NIBC, TBST, TH, TNTC] in action [Hie, Lns], which ensures final victory [BNTC, Hie, NIBC].
g. ἐξουσία (LN 37.35, 76.12) (BAGD 2. p. 278): 'authority' [AB, BNTC, Lns, WBC; all versions except KJV, NAB], 'authority to rule' [LN (37.35)], 'power' [Alf, BAGD, LN (76.12); KJV, NAB]. It refers to God's freedom of action as Creator [BNTC, EBC, Hie, Law], his sovereignty and lordship [Lg, TH, TNTC, WBC], his right and power to rule [Lns, TBST], his ability to meet all human needs [NIBC].

QUESTION—What relationship is indicated by the phrase μόνῳ θεῷ σωτῆρι ἡμῶν 'to the only God our Savior'?

It is in apposition with τῷ δυναμένῳ... 'to the one being able . . . ' in verse 24 and expands the description by characterizing God's uniqueness [Hie]. The use of ἡμῶν 'our' here and in the following phrase unites the author with his readers and implies their close relationship with the Father and the Son [Hie].

QUESTION—What is the phrase διὰ Ἰησοῦ Χριστοῦ τοῦ κυρίου ἡμῶν 'through Jesus Christ our Lord' connected with?

It is directed against those who reject Christ's lordship [Law, Lg(M)].

JUDE 1:25

1. It is connected with σωτῆρι ἡμῶν 'our Savior' [AB, Hie, Hu, Law, Lg, Lns, TNTC; NET]: God saves us through Jesus Christ.
2. It is connected with the following phrase δόξα κτλ. 'glory (etc.)' [BNTC, EGT, ICC, TBST; CEV, NAB, NIV, NLT, REB]: glory . . . to God through Jesus Christ.

QUESTION—What verb is implied in this verse?
1. It is the imperative ἔστω 'let there be' or optative εἴη 'may there be' [AB, Alf, Lg, NIBC; all versions except CEV, NLT]: let/may glory (etc.) be ascribed to God our Savior.
2. An indicative verb εἰσιν 'are/belong' is to be supplied [BNTC, EBC, El, Hu, Law, TBST, TNTC, WBC; CEV, NLT]: glory (etc.) are/belong to God. The indicative is required because of the reference to eternity past [TNTC, WBC].
3. Both concepts are included [EGT]: glory (etc.) belong to God, and may they be ever more fully realized.
4. It is an exclamation of praise which does not require an expressed verb [Hie, ICC, Lns].

before[a] all the age[b] and now and into[c] all the ages.[d] Amen.[e]

a. πρό with genitive object (LN 67.17) (BAGD 2. p. 701): 'before' [AB, Alf, BAGD, BNTC, LN, Lns, WBC; CEV, ISV, NET, NIV, NJB, NRSV, REB, TNT], 'from' [TEV].
b. αἰών (LN **67.133**, 67.143): 'age, era' [LN (67.143)], 'eon' [Lns], 'time' [Alf, BNTC, WBC; ISV, NET, NRSV, REB, TNT], 'time began' [CEV]. This singular noun is translated as a plural: 'ages' [AB; NIV, NJB], 'ages past' [TEV]. The phrase πρὸ παντὸς τοῦ αἰῶνος 'before all the age' is translated 'before time began' [CEV], 'since all ages past' [LN (67.133)], 'from ages past' [NAB], 'in the beginning' [NLT]. This phrase implies eternity past [Alf, Hie]; it is included as adoring worship rather than as a prayer [Hie].
c. εἰς with accusative object (LN 84.22): 'into' [LN], 'for' [BNTC, Lns, WBC; NAB, REB, TNT], 'to' [Alf].
d. αἰών (LN 67.95, 67.143): 'age' [Alf, BNTC, LN (67.143)], 'era' [LN (67.143)], 'eon' [Lns]. The phrase εἰς πάντας τοὺς αἰῶνας 'into all the ages' is translated 'ever' [KJV], 'forever' [AB; NJB, NRSV], 'forever and ever' [LN (67.95); TEV], 'for evermore' [WBC; CEV, NIV, NLT, REB], 'for all eternity' [ISV, NET, TNT], 'for ages to come' [NAB]. This phrase implies future eternity [Alf, Hie].
e. ἀμήν (LN 72.6) (BAGD 1. p. 45): 'amen' [AB, Alf, BAGD, BNTC, Lns, WBC; all versions], 'so let it be' [BAGD], 'truly' [BAGD, LN], 'indeed' [LN]. It means 'so be it' [BNTC, Hie, NIBC, NTC, TH].

QUESTION—What relationship is indicated by this entire phrase?
It emphatically indicates eternity—past, present, and future [Law]; it indicates the author's belief in the pre-existence and eternity of Christ [ICC].

QUESTION—What relationship is indicated by the phrase πρὸ παντὸς τοῦ αἰῶνος 'before all the age'?

It refers to eternity before time began [Hie, Lns, TH; CEV, REB, TNT]; it declares the eternal pre-existence of Christ [Hie, Lg(M)]

www.ingramcontent.com/pod-product-compliance
Lightning Source LLC
Chambersburg PA
CBHW070339240426